# FAST
# FORWARD

## Josh Herring

# CONTENTS

# ACKNOWLEDGEMENTS

This book would not be possible without my best friend, my Lord Jesus. Everything I have was given to me by him. I would like to thank my wife Jenee for her unwavering love and support our entire marriage and for helping me raise our four beautiful children: Jude, Jhett, Jade, and Jaxton. They truly make my life complete and I am the most blessed man on the planet. I would also like to honor my parents Ron and Cindy Herring for the unending love and guidance they have given me my entire life.

I would like to thank my pastor, Brian Kinsey for his wisdom, counsel, and love for our family. Also it was an immense honor having him write the foreward for this book.

To my elders, Bishop Stan Gleason, Bishop James Stark, Bishop Darrell Johns, and Bishop. C. P Williams, I honor you and thank you for always being there for me.

I would like to thank my editor Patricia Bollmann for the hours she spent correcting the many mistakes I had made.

To my friend, and graphics designer, Ryan Johns thank you for your amazing work and friendship.

I would like to thank Dust Jacket publishing company for all of their help in publishing this effort.

To my many friends who have requested and kept prompting to me write a book on the subject of fasting, I thank you also.

# FOREWORD

In this day and hour, fasting is more important than ever before, yet it is a weapon in our arsenal that is often over-looked. Josh Herring brings his experience and insight to this critical subject, explaining the significance of fasting and its impact on advancing God's kingdom. The result is living a godly life that will have an eternal impact on others and the church. For this reason, fasting has been an integral part of my ministry for the past fifty years.

Studying the Bible nourishes and strengthens our spirit, but fasting prepares us for spiritual warfare. When practiced together, prayer and fasting forge a powerful weapon against the enemy. As Herring explains, "The rewards of fasting far outweigh the benefits of feasting." God designed fasting to challenge us and elevate our relationship with him to create powerful breakthroughs in the Spirit. As the author says, food can distract us from the greatest encounters we could ever have with God.

Fasting will help us change and grow and move to the next level. We will draw closer to God and feel more compassion for those suffering. These are just a few of the twelve rewards of fasting as presented in Isaiah 58. In Fast Forward, Herring counsels the reader to "develop spiritual habits that will challenge you. Go beyond your devotions. If it does not challenge you, it will not change you."

Desperation drove biblical heroes to deny their flesh by fasting, because, as Herring states, "Nothing will cause one to go on a fast like a desperate need." Esther fasted for the deliverance of the Jews. As a result, she gained wisdom, confidence, and strength to intercede before the king for her people. Daniel fasted for an answer to prayer even though the answer was resisted by the demonic prince of Persia. Nehemiah fasted to restore Jerusalem during the threat of constant war. Finally, the entire city of Nineveh fasted and repented when they heard of God's impending judgment from the preaching of Jonah.

Fasting sets spiritual forces in motion to encourage and empower, enabling us to defeat the enemy and accomplish the mission. Fasting fine-tunes our focus and opens the door to our destiny, thus impacting not only our lives but the lives of everyone around us. As you read this book, say yes to the Spirit. Begin your fasting with an expectation that God will move and that you will develop a deeper, more intimate relationship with him that no opposition can stop.

–Brian Kinsey, pastor of
First Pentecostal Church, Pensacola
Author of *Made for More:
7 Proven Strategies for
Reaching Your Full Potential*

# INTRODUCTION

There simply is no substitute for it, no alternative formula that will yield the same results, no other avenue of spiritual consecration that will lead you into this dimension and reveal the deeper things of the Spirit. It is the sacrifice heaven rewards the most, hell fears the most, and humans hate the most. I am, of course, speaking about fasting.

If you've been searching for answers and have failed to find them, fasting will diminish the devil's power and open up divine direction and supernatural instruction like nothing else can. Fasting will kill the flesh like no other sacrificial endeavor, which is why we dislike even the thought of fasting.

Let's face it: we love to eat! But we don't live to eat; that is, until we start skipping meals. Then our stomach begins to growl, demanding a renegotiation that cancels out our self-denial. Fasting is a hard-won battle because our flesh wants to be in control. In this book, with the help of the Lord, I'm going to lead you on a journey that will inspire you to fight this inward battle and come out of it victoriously.

There are many reasons to go on a fast, and we will get to as many of them as we can in this book. But for now, if you need deliverance from any addictions, habits, or strongholds in your life, I challenge you to fast about them. Nothing breaks chains like a consecrated fast. When done properly, fasting can even restore health to a sick or diseased body.

If there is a generational curse in your family, you can banish it forever. You can force hell out of your life by pursuing the Lord so intensely through fasting and prayer that demons would rather flee from you and your family than hang around and suffer the blows dealt by each meal you say no to.

Some people have little or no concept of the meaning of fasting. In a nutshell, to fast means to abstain from food; to eat very little or abstain from certain foods. It is a time of self-denial. We will discuss different types of fasts for the purpose of motivating even the weakest among us to "go for it" to attain a relationship with Jesus like they've never known before. I truly feel the greatest benefit of fasting is that it brings an individual close to Jesus. Nothing else compares to feeling and knowing he is closer to you than he's ever been before. Fasting and prayer will lead you to a secret place in the Lord that can't be found any other way.

> *But thou, when thou fastest, anoint thine head, and wash thy face; that thou appear not unto men to fast, but unto thy Father which is in secret: and thy Father, which seeth in secret shall reward thee openly.* (Matt. 6:17–18)

Fasting will cause you to ask for incredible things you never dreamed of asking the Lord for. Moses asked to see the glory of the Lord, and his request was granted. He saw things we've only read about in scripture. Moses' supernatural experience still blows me away today! (See Exod. 33:18–23.)

Have you ever wondered how we know the events of creation? After all, there were no humans standing around taking notes on their iPads. There were no cell phones recording the voice of the

Creator when he thundered, "Let there be light!" The answer came in response to Moses' request during a fast. The Lord said, "Thou shalt see my back parts."

> *And the Lord said, Behold there is a place by me, and thou shalt stand upon a rock: and it shall come to pass, while my glory passeth by, that I will put thee in a clift of the rock, and will cover thee with my hand while I pass by: and I will take away mine hand, and thou shalt see my back parts: but my face shall not be seen.* (Exod. 33:21–23)

According to the Old Testament Hebrew Lexicon King James Version, the word for "back parts" is 'achowr, meaning the backward, behind, hinder part, or hereafter (of time). Thus, many theologians believe that through this supernatural experience God revealed to Moses the events that took place during creation. What a moment, what a miracle, what a memory!

You might be thinking, "Yeah, well, he was Moses and I'm not, so why should I go on a fast? What supernatural event could possibly take place if I fast?" Well, my fellow believer, I am ecstatic that you are asking! First, the deep things of God are out there, just beyond your reach. They're in a world you've never acknowledged or maybe even known about. Second, if you don't reach for these things, someone else is going to see, hear, feel, and experience them. It might as well be you!

In this book I will share several personal miracles and experiences I've witnessed either during or as a result of fasting. I promise that as you read this book you're going to want to leave the dishes in the cupboard and the silverware in the drawer and go on an extended fast. I guarantee you will find more of Jesus than you have currently experienced, and God's word will open up to you like never before. As you decrease, he will increase in ways you never imagined! Are you ready? Are you willing? Anything is possible, so why wait any longer? Let's fast forward!

# CHAPTER 1

## Signals to Fast

It was November 30, 2008, when the signal came. My wife, Jenee, and I were living in Millington, Tennessee. We had been married only about six months and were evangelizing together full time. Prior to our marriage I had been evangelizing almost five years, and up to then my schedule usually had filled up months in advance. But in November 2008 a desert season blew in. I hadn't preached in two weeks; I wasn't scheduled anywhere for the next two Sundays; there were no calls or texts containing invitations to preach. The signal started flashing in my spirit and mind that I needed to go on a fast. If we were to survive this dry season, I had to do something besides just sit still and hope for the best.

I heard the signal loud and clear: "Go on a ten-day fast and the Lord will bring you out of this." The longest fast I had ever completed prior to receiving this signal was eight days, and it had taken me years to accomplish it. I previously had attempted to go on extended fasts only to stop after five, six, seven, or eight days. But this time I knew we needed direction and there was only one way to get it: my flesh was going to have to die on an altar for more than just a day or two.

I started the next day—December first—determined that nothing was going to stop me from finding out what the Lord was trying to tell me. We were so strapped financially during those ten days that I probably would've had to fast regardless. While I searched for an answer from God, Jenee survived on the only food we had in our cupboard: canned green beans and canned tuna.

Time crawled by for seven days with no answer—but also no doubt that one was coming. Then came day eight, the barrier day, the day I had ended previous unfulfilled fasts. A little voice started chirping incessantly in my mind: "Nothing's going to change, so why don't you just eat and say you tried?" I knew that voice; I'd heard it before. But on that eighth day I knew I had to ignore that voice—because there's nothing worse than going all out for a spiritual cause for a little while and then backing out. It injects one's spirit with self-defeat, discouragement, and unease. I was determined not to give up.

Day nine marked the entrance into new territory, and I knew God was watching and listening. I can testify to the truth of the prophet Isaiah's statement that perfect peace prevails when a person's mind is stayed on God. Because something happened at the end of the ninth day I will never forget.

The phone rang. It was a pastor from Florida calling to inquire if we would be interested in moving to that state and basing our evangelistic ministry out of his church. He had a beautiful condo we could live in; we could load up our stuff and move in whenever we wanted! I could've jumped through the phone line and hugged him. Here was living proof that God had heard me!

Still, I fasted the tenth day just to be sure this answer was from the Lord, and he confirmed that it was his will. Do you think that call would've come if had I ignored the signal to go on a fast? No, I don't either.

We gave away almost everything we had and loaded our little Toyota Camry to the gills. By the end of December we had emerged out of that desert wasteland and into a harvest season such as we had never experienced. Over the next few years, we saw over two thousand people get baptized in the name of Jesus. Revival broke out everywhere we went.

If you are searching for direction from the Lord, the best thing you can do is go on a fast, because it will position you to hear his voice. Think of it as listening to a radio station. Sometimes the static is so loud it drowns out anything else in the room and you can't think clearly. Fasting dials down that statical volume. It silences the distractions of life, the mind, and the enemy, enabling you to hear God's voice like a clarion call.

Thus I learned by experience that a desperate need for direction will set off a signal in the Spirit to go on an extended fast. Direction from the Lord is hinged upon your sensitivity to his voice and his will, and nothing will make you more sensitive to the Spirit than fasting. I believe that fasting, combined with prayer, is the ultimate navigator of your life, your calling, your ministry, and any other opportunities that may arise in your future.

Following is a list of five signals that tell you it's time to go on an extended fast. If you will heed these signals, the positive rewards will blow your mind.

## SPIRITUAL FRUSTRATION

First let me clarify what spiritual frustration is not: it is not Holy Ghost indignation, where the Spirit of the Lord rises up in you in disagreement with rebellion or evil that is around you. That's not spiritual frustration; it's godly frustration. One biblical example is Lot living in the wicked city of Sodom. He "was a righteous man who was sick of the shameful immorality of the wicked people around him. Yes, Lot was a righteous man who was tormented in his soul by the wickedness he saw and heard day after day" (2 Pet. 2:7–8, NLT). The spiritual frustration I'm referring to happens when our flesh begins to get in the way of spiritual things. It causes us to become distracted and upset with situations or people in our lives to the extent we stop progressing toward God and start regressing away from God.

If you are feeling exhausted from the fight of life or if you feel like you're going in circles and nothing is exciting you anymore, it's time to fast. Spiritual frustration, if not dealt with effectually and quickly, will reap negative results. Some of the most bitter attitudes toward others are found in spiritually frustrated people. Spiritual frustration can wrest your eyes away from your own course and shift your focus to someone else's blessings. Then you wonder why those people are so connected or have so much favor, because you're the one who deserves the recognition or the position.

Becoming mired in spiritual frustration can open the door to demonic spirits and human emotions that will cripple a believer's walk with God. Nothing invites evil spirits into someone's life more than a door left ajar through bitterness! For instance, bitterness can lead to anger and hatred if not dealt with through prayer and fasting. If you are bitter over another person's good fortune, go on a fast to clear your vision and help you focus on what will move you forward in God.

In fact, fasting will renew your mind and correct your thinking in all areas of life. It clears away the clutter and cuts out the confusion in your spirit, enabling you to become all that you can be for the Lord. Fasting will even enable you to forgive people against whom you weren't aware that you harbored ill feelings. Like an anchor chain drawing up an anchor, fasting will bring subjects and people to the surface of your mind so you can deal with them. The longer you fast the more frustration dwindles until it is replaced by the expectation of greater things waiting for you in the future.

One of the reasons I'm such a believer in fasting is that it erases my frustrations and helps me refocus on things that really matter. For one thing, fasting causes me to look into the mirror of my own life and highlights negative emotions and flaws. Unfortunately, we tend to resent and/or ignore constructive criticism from others who can see areas in our life that need correcting or tweaking, but they are afraid we won't receive their constructive criticism and the relationship will suffer or even be severed. Fasting highlights these issues so we can deal with them privately with the Lord's help. We all say we want to become better. Well, here's a way to do it: fast that frustration away. Open yourself up to becoming all you can be in Jesus.

## CARNALITY

Carnality is another strong signal that a fast is necessary. We all have carnal moments where we say or think something we later regret, but a good prayer meeting can usually take care of those moments. However, there is another dimension of carnality that needs to be overcome with a fast. This dimension is carnality that occurs (1) when you'd rather do anything but pray; (2) when you don't think of picking up your Bible to do some daily reading until you've closed your eyes for the night; (3) when godly things don't attract your attention anymore; (4) when being on social media for hours checking the statuses of others is fine, but reading the Bible for five minutes makes you sleepy. If you're experiencing these or any number of other symptoms of carnality, I strongly suggest a fast!

Don't let carnality keep you distracted for months or years. When you catch yourself being tempted and not being convicted or when questionable thoughts don't just pass through your mind but instead take up residence, it's time to fast!

*This I say then, Walk in the Spirit, and ye shall not fulfil the lust of the flesh.* (Gal. 5:16)

There's no greater threat to hell than a man or woman who leaves carnality behind and walks in the Spirit. The kingdom of darkness is wary of that person every moment of the day. Hell fears the fast-er, the one who isn't satisfied with tapping into the Spirit once in a while but instead walks and lives in the Spirit. There's a major difference between tapping into the Spirit and walking in the Spirit.

Tapping into the Spirit includes things like focusing on God when you're about to preach, sing, or be used at a certain event or meeting. It includes a sudden desire to be used in the gifts of the Spirit despite not being totally consecrated that day, or a need to feel God in a desperate situation when there has been no effort of late to reach him. Basically, tapping into the Spirit is pursuing God part time while taking frequent spiritual breaks (i.e., carnality). Many people who are used mightily can move in the Spirit when they're behind a pulpit or holding a microphone but not necessarily when they're on the street or in the store. These are classic examples of tapping into the Spirit.

Walking in the Spirit is different from tapping into it occasionally. Walking in the Spirit includes daily commitment to prayer and reading the word along with a day set aside each week for fasting. The fruit of the Spirit in one's life also is a good indicator of a spiritual walk. To the list of spiritual fruit in Galatians 5:22–23 (love, joy, peace, forbearance, kindness, goodness, faithfulness, gentleness, and self-control), Paul later added compassion and humility (Col. 3:12, NIV). Fasting truly will kill the flesh, allowing the precious fruit of the Spirit to flourish in your life.

Picture a chalk outline of your body. Inside the white outline is a thin black layer called the spirit. The rest is a red shape of your body called the flesh (carnal nature). This is how most of us live—a carnal nature covered over by a thin layer of spirit. Now picture that red flesh (carnality) shrinking and becoming smaller and smaller inside the chalked outline as the black spirit-layer gets larger and larger. That is what happens when you go on a fast; your spirit increases as the flesh decreases. Fasting will shrink not only your human flesh but your carnality as well. The more of God's Spirit that lives in you the easier it becomes to give up the willfulness of your carnal nature and submit to God's will and divine nature.

Flesh that is never crucified through fasting will eventually fill up not only the inside of the chalked outline, but ultimately will ooze outside the line for all to see. If you were to examine yourself today, would you find the Spirit of the Lord consuming you or would you find that red flesh taking over your life? When you arrive at the answer, you'll know if you need to go on a fast.

Fasting reveals the real you and then puts that version of you on an altar and says you will never be like this again. Fasting will change your life forever, especially if you do it often. Nothing is as powerful; nothing is as important!

## PHYSICAL SIGNALS

Another signal that you need to go on a fast isn't necessarily as spiritual as it is physical. If you are experiencing health issues, fasting can be an incredible source of healing. One of the many types of fasting is a juice fast, during which you drink only freshly made juices and water for a duration of time. This can provide several benefits for the physical body because it gives your internal organs a rest from all the pumping and digesting. If you are having digestive issues, go on a fast and come off it properly, and you will see dramatic improvement.

Isaiah 58 is known to many Bible readers as the "fasting chapter." In it you will find two important things: (1) a description of the fast that pleases the Lord, and (2) a promise of some of the rewards a person can expect from obeying God's word. I suggest reading this chapter if the idea of going on a fast is tugging at your heart. One of the rewards you can expect is that health will return to your body.

*Then your light shall break forth like the morning, your healing shall spring forth speedily, and your righteousness shall go before you; the glory of the Lord shall be your rear guard.* (Isa. 58:8, NKJV)

This isn't just my opinion; the word says you can expect your health to return speedily. In my own experience, I was suffering from a painful knot in one of my back muscles. After I went on a lengthy fast, the knot shrank drastically and the pain diminished. I also have seen and heard of tumors shrinking when one goes on a fast. This is true especially with lengthy fasts. Obviously, if you've eaten junk food, fried food, and sugary food for twenty years it is going to take more than twenty-four hours of abstinence to fix the effects of those bad habits on your internal organs.

A word of warning: One of the things people tend to do when they come off of a lengthy fast is to gorge on sugars and other carbohydrates to satisfy the craving that has been ignored for days, and in some cases, weeks. I've made that mistake before and learned that binging after fasting actually reverses your healing. It can damage your stomach and slow your metabolic rate to the degree that the body will automatically store the junk foods as fat, creating an energy reserve in the event of future starvation. The best way to avoid this negative effect is to come off of the fast slowly and carefully. We will discuss this in greater detail later in the book.

## EMOTIONAL SIGNALS

Another signal that it's time to go on a fast is not physical, but rather emotional. If you're struggling with depression, oppression, fear, anxiety, stress, fatigue, feeling overwhelmed by the cares of life, or all of the above, I encourage you not to surrender to these negative feelings but rather to stand up and fight! Life itself can oppress you, and then hell dumps more junk on top of the load you're already carrying. Remember that chirping voice I mentioned earlier in the chapter? That voice will insist, "Nothing's ever going to get better. Besides, you've done so many wrong things that you deserve this bad outcome or this trial." Keep entertaining the wrong voices and you can become extremely depressed, even suicidal.

There is an answer that can bring your mind and emotions out of the darkness—fast yourself out! Your mind may be in torment, but if you make a decision right now to go on that fast, things are going to change for the better. I believe with all my heart that fasting ushers in acute mental focus and brings one out of any type of emotional trauma. If you were hurt in life by someone, even if it was years ago, fasting can heal your troubled mind and bleeding heart. Fasting can enable you to forgive the worst of people.

How can this be? When a wounded child of God begins to fast, God intervenes. No matter the pain, fasting can work its way inside of it and heal it from the inside out. God wants to free you from this emotional baggage. Let's go back to the "fasting chapter" for proof.

*Is not this the fast that I have chosen? to loose the bands of wickedness, to undo the heavy burdens, and to let the oppressed go free, and that ye break every yoke?* (Isa. 58:6)

Embedded in this verse are some of the emotional benefits to fasting. One benefit is that God lets the oppressed go free. The Hebrew word for "oppressed" is ratsats, meaning to crush or to be crushed, bruised, broken, or discouraged. In other words, if you are broken or crushed by a situation or circumstance, fasting sets you free of that.

Isaiah further stated that fasting breaks every yoke. The Hebrew word for "breaks" is nathaq, meaning to pull or to tear off, to lift, and to root out. Whatever yoke is choking you, fasting will tear it off, lift it off, or, my personal favorite, root it out. It doesn't matter who put the yoke on you or how long it's been there. It doesn't matter how heavy it is or if there are multiple yokes. Fasting will tear all of them off. Fasting goes beneath the surface of your smiling face, delves down deep to the source of the pain, and demands deliverance!

God is offering you hope as you read this. He wants to put a smile on your face that isn't masking pain or fear. He wants you to feel real happiness, not the fraudulent expressions of joy that are nothing more than a cover-up of something that needs to be healed in your spirit, mind, or heart. You need to experience the peace that is above and beyond any human peace of mind. It is God's peace. He said in his word that he would keep us in perfect peace if our mind is stayed on him. I want that peace. I have experienced that peace. That peace comes through prayer and fasting and meditating on his word. You can experience it today!

Every person needs love, no matter how independent he or she may seem. Love is a balm that heals the deepest wounds and removes the greatest regrets. People are suffering in silence and convincing themselves there is no way their problem can be fixed. I refuse to sit back and let people suffer without trying to shine a beacon of love and hope their way. I want to show them the way out so they can be free, so they can experience a better life, the life God has for them. The life only he knows they can have because he came to earth and paid for it with his own precious blood on the cross. (See Acts 20:28; Heb. 9:12.)

## FASTING FOR OTHERS

This is perhaps the weakest of all spiritual signals, yet it's the signal that can bring the most miraculous results. Why is this a difficult signal to pick up? Because this dimension of sensitivity requires a selfless, humble, kingdom-minded individual. To fast for someone else is to be Christlike. For example, Jesus did not fast for forty days in the wilderness for himself; he was fasting for all of humanity's needs he was about to face head-on. The blind, the deaf, the lame, the poor, and the lost were going to come to him for help. There would even be encounters with the dead who needed to be raised. Every needy person who would come to Jesus would have their needs met because they were encountering the one who had fasted for them. Fasting for someone else is a secret that few people ever pursue.

Fasting for others will yield rewards for them as well as for yourself. For instance, God turned Job's captivity when he prayed for his friends. When he prayed for them, God said, "That is enough, Satan. Release Job from any more pain, trials, loss, and problems." If simply praying for them turned his situation around, what do you think fasting will do when you look at the burdens of others and say, "Not my will, but thine be done, Lord."

Many people in the Bible besides Jesus knew this secret of fasting for others: Moses, Esther, Nehemiah, Daniel, John the Baptist, Paul, and the list goes on. In the ninth chapter of Matthew Jesus encapsulated a discussion on fasting with the healing of a paralytic, the raising of a dead girl, the healing of a sick woman, and the healing of the blind and the mute. The rewards of fasting for others are miraculous!

Is there someone who needs you to touch God on their behalf? Is someone in a financial crisis? Is someone fighting a spirit of suicide? More to the point, do you even care? If there's no reward for you, will you undertake the assignment? Or are you more selfish than you realize? The strange thing is that some of us will pray for the gifts of the Spirit to operate in our lives where we can see the miraculous flow, but we won't fast in private for someone else. Do you desire the platform and not the altar? Are you seeking validation and recognition from others for a spiritual gift that isn't yours to begin with? Lord, help us to become truly kingdom minded! Help us to see the needs of others as clearly as we see our own.

Someone near you is waiting for you to get connected to the Spirit. Someone needs you to go to the throne room on their behalf. What if you were the one needing access to God? Wouldn't you want someone to carry your need before his magnificent presence where every knee bows and every tongue confesses that he, Jesus, is Lord over all?

Heaven is waiting for your response, hell fears your response, and someone near you hopes for your response: "Yes, I will sacrifice for you. I will push the plate back so you can be healed. I will deny myself so God will meet your need." It is imperative that you understand these signals before moving on to the next chapter.

## CHAPTER 2

# How Badly Do You Want It?

How badly do you want it? That's the question I ask everyone who tells me they have a desire to find more of God than they've ever known, because some things from the Lord come only to those who hunger after them and do whatever it is he asks them to do. Anyone can talk about wanting a closer walk with God, but where I come from—Alaska—talk is cheap. You need an unquenchable, burning fire inside of you that will not let go, that never lets you feel satisfied with what you've already experienced.

The nation of Israel resisted everything Jeremiah prophesied. They hated him for his predictions of disaster that would befall them if they didn't heed the voice of the Lord. Throughout the years of Jeremiah's ministry, they acted out their intense hatred of him in various ways: he was whipped and put in stocks (20:1–3); he was attacked by a mob (26:1–9); he was threatened by the enraged king who had just read Jeremiah's scroll (36:26); he was arrested, beaten, accused of treason, and thrown in jail (37:1–15); from jail he was thrown into a muddy cistern and left to starve (38:1–6); and he was rejected by his own family members (12:6).

Jeremiah had been hearing prophetic words in his ears since he was a child. But after years of chipping away at the people's stony hearts and receiving nothing but abuse for his efforts, vultures of doubt began circling in his mind and ministry. He was through. He declared he wouldn't mention the Lord or speak anymore in his name. How could anyone blame him for quitting?

In today's world, most people would consider Jeremiah's ministry a failure, because they think if people in ministry are not popular or prosperous, they must be doing something wrong and few will listen to them. I dare say that if Jeremiah were alive today, no one would be booking him for their next conference. He was too forceful, too blunt, too irritating, and his words hit too close to home.

But the Lord wouldn't let this disheartened prophet quit. Jeremiah described it like this: "His message becomes like a fire locked up inside of me, burning in my heart and soul. I grow weary of holding it in; I cannot contain it" (Jer. 20:9, NET). Despite the criticisms bombarding him on the outside, the fire of the Lord's message was still blazing on the inside, and he couldn't just walk away. He was a warrior, and warriors don't quit.

Have you ever wanted something so badly you would do almost anything to acquire it? If you look back far enough, there probably has been a moment when you were desperate for something to happen, for someone to notice you, or for an answer to a burning question that wouldn't let go. That is how it works in the Spirit as well. The Lord places a desire in your life for more, and you begin to hunger for it with a passion that hell fears. God will give you a taste of something miraculous and powerful and then watch to see how you react to the taste.

## WILL YOU PAY THE PRICE?

If you walk into an ice cream parlor or frozen yogurt shop, you will see an array of wonderful flavors. Most of these establishments offer free samples. This usually calls for the employee to pull out from behind the counter a spoon the size of your average thumbnail and a thimble-size cup, and then ask which flavor you want to sample. Once you've tasted the treat, you are then faced with a decision: you can either be satisfied with the tiny free sample and leave the establishment, or you can purchase a much larger portion. In other words, the thimbleful is free but the bowlful will cost you something. There is a price to wanting a greater portion.

It is the same in the spirit world. You can cherish the memory of that moment in the past when you heard something amazing or saw something miraculous, or you can get something current and far more wonderful by paying the price. How do you pay the price? Fasting and prayer—a lot of it.

## MAKE THE DEPOSIT NOW

Another illustration comes in the form of a bank account. If you make periodic deposits into your account and then the day comes when you need extra funds to purchase something, there's no stress because the money has accumulated in your account. Fasting is like making a deposit, and a prayer request is like making a withdrawal. If you fast enough, you will have more than you need when it's time for a spiritual withdrawal.

David, while preparing to fight the undefeated Goliath, stopped by a brook, gathered five smooth stones, and put them in his bag. It turned out he needed only one of those stones to knock Goliath off his feet. The point is this: If David had missed on his first throw, he would have had four more chances to strike his target. Why? Because he took the time beforehand to stock up on extra ammunition. That's what fasting is and does. The more you fast the more ammunition you have in your arsenal.

I have yet to see a child of God who routinely fasts end up being the underdog when a fight breaks out for their destiny in the spirit world. They might be overlooked by people (because people look on the outward appearance), but hell is well aware that the one who fasts will likely be the victor in every battle, simply because of the ammunition they possess in the Spirit. The devil and all his angels know the difficulty of overpowering a fasting warrior. Warriors who are fasting have tenacity; they would rather do anything than eat. They know what is at stake and they know how to get the job done.

It is ironic that people are usually impressed by personality but heaven is moved by sacrifice. It also is ironic that people who fast often live in the shadow of charismatic personalities. However, when the devil shows up for battle and comes face to face with the fast-er, he's going to wish he had never stepped onto that battlefield.

## YOU WILL WANT TO FAST!

I stand behind the claim that the hungrier people are for God the more likely they are going to want to fast. But let's get one thing straight: fasting is not fun. It means placing yourself on a grueling, bloody altar that demands death. Flesh must die through fasting. However, people who are hungry for God see this altar as more than a death sentence to the desires of their "old man"; they see it as the opportunity for more of Jesus to be manifested in their lives. To the hungry servants of the Lord, it is a blessing to fast. It is an honor to say no to the invitation to the banquet table so the Spirit can thrive and dominate the outcomes of situations that arise in their lives.

When people ask me what they should do about their hunger or craving for certain foods while on a fast, I ask them how serious the need is that they're fasting about. That burger can wait if the need hasn't been answered yet. The talking pizza that keeps interrupting your sleep urging, "You need to eat me!" is lying. It is a ploy of hell to see if you're serious. By the way, the longer you dwell on tantalizing thoughts of pepperoni, cheese, and a choice of three toppings, the more likely you are going to end the fast. In contrast, the longer you say, "No thank you!" to the marinara dream, the more likely you are connecting yourself to the reality of the miracle dream the Lord placed in your spirit.

## PRIORITIES OR PLEASURE

Many of us are like spiritual Esaus; we sell out a powerfully anointed future in the will of God for a bowl of food. We settle for less from the Spirit than what we could have had because we just can't imagine not eating for a few days or weeks. Why can't we imagine it? Because we aren't in tune enough to comprehend everything the Lord has for us. It's easy to just go ahead and eat when we're oblivious to the potential positive results of our sacrifice. Some of us need to audibly tell ourselves, "No, you aren't going to eat today. There's something far too valuable at stake to be replaced by a steak!"

Esau would have done well to heed this advice when he came in from the fields and caught the aroma of baking bread and simmering pottage on Jacob's camp fire. It was easy for him to let go of his birthright because all he could think about was satisfying his hunger. Thus he "showed contempt for his rights as firstborn" (Gen. 35:34, NLT), or, as stated in The Message, he "shrugged off his rights." He thought the casual trade wouldn't matter because he was still the firstborn, which, he assumed, would entitle him to receive a double portion.

Let's look more closely at the implications of Esau's sellout. In patriarchal times a "birthright" came into effect upon the death of the father. The younger sons each received an equal portion of their father's goods, but the firstborn received a double portion. The firstborn also inherited the leadership of the family; in effect, he became the patriarch or the priest of the family clan. Apart from the firstborn's entitlement to the birthright, each son received a blessing—a pronouncement by the father to his sons of what he envisioned for their lives. A greater blessing, of course, was pronounced over the firstborn.

Perhaps Esau wasn't so much concerned about the birthright as much as he was about the blessing. Maybe he didn't care for the responsibilities that came along with the birthright. To him, the birthright wasn't as appealing as the blessing. I know a lot of people who love the blessings of popularity and prosperity but want nothing to do with that birthright. But Jacob was the polar opposite. He didn't even mention the blessing that day when Esau staggered in, hungry from the hunt. Jacob wanted that birthright.

If you look at it from the spiritual point of view, the birthright is the power to oversee the favor of God. It is entrusted to your care by your heavenly Father. If you don't want the responsibility, someone else does, and they will do what it takes to get it. If Esau had waited to eat just a little bit longer, if he had gone into his own tent and made himself something to eat or asked one of the servants to prepare it, he wouldn't have thrown away this part of his future.

Be careful when the flesh says, "I can't go another hour without something to eat!" when the Spirit is telling you to endure a little longer. You may end up regretting what you hand over to someone else for their future, leaving you to wonder what your future would have been like if only you had that birthright.

Why does the Bible say God "hated" Esau? (See Rom. 9:13; cf. Mal. 1:2.) According to the Apostolic Study Bible, this statement doesn't mean God detested Esau; "rather, it is an idiomatic expression indicating choice or preference and means, 'I have chosen Jacob instead of Esau.'" Why did God choose the younger son over the elder? Was it because of Esau's character flaw? Hebrews 12:16 identifies his character flaw as profaneness. Other Bible translations render the word as lacking reverence for the things of God, unholy, or, as The Message calls it, "the Esau syndrome." God didn't hate Esau; he hated Esau's carelessness and godless attitude. The man didn't care about the birthright because he couldn't wait another five minutes to eat. God hates it when he gives us the ability to sacrifice or to endure and we take it lightly and hand it off to somebody else.

That day when Esau squandered his birthright, he had no clue that someday he would also lose the blessing to Jacob and be left with next to nothing. Had he known that fact, he never would have stopped by Jacob's campfire. I believe that some of us, if we knew the ramifications of our compromising ways, would be quick to say, "No, I can't afford to eat this and lose divine favor. I have too many eternal things to look forward to only to enjoy something temporal that will cause me to forfeit what I can have in God."

Why does the Bible say God loved Jacob? Because Jacob's hunger was far different than Esau's. Esau was hungry for immediate gratification—food to satisfy his grumbling stomach; Jacob was hungry for more than just the portion he would receive as a younger son. He wanted the exceptional privileges of his brother. To add to the drama, the family had given him a name that means supplanter or deceiver or, literally, "to follow at the heel." Perhaps he was given that name because immediately after birth Jacob had grasped his twin brother's heel. Or perhaps it was because of the prophecy that was pronounced over the twins before they were born that the elder would serve the younger. In any case, the name began to haunt Jacob's character and he became the embodiment of its meaning.

The day Esau showed up at his cooking fire, Jacob saw an opportunity to go after the birthright. Then, when it came time to bestow the blessing on Esau, Jacob deceived their aged father by impersonating his twin brother. Isaac, whose eyesight was dim, suspected something was amiss, but Jacob finally convinced him and the old man gave his younger son the blessing that rightfully belonged to the elder son.

Certainly, in the beginning Jacob's methods were wrong; he used craftiness to get what he wanted. But twenty years later, after one encounter with an angel, he was a changed man. From then on, he obtained what he wanted through spiritual means. He wrestled so tenaciously with the angel that the angel couldn't get free. Jacob said, "I will not let you go unless you bless me!" The angel asked, "What is your name?" Perhaps Jacob was reluctant or even ashamed when he replied, "Jacob."

The angel pronounced, "Your name will no longer be Jacob. From now on you will be called Israel because you have fought with God and with men and have won." (See Gen. 32:26–28, NLT.) The supplanter's new name was "Israel," a name with many nuances of meaning and theological significance. Various Bible dictionaries and commentaries have defined the name as upright, straight, righteous, happy, blessed. The Dictionary of Old Testament Proper Names defines Israel as "He will be prince with God" or "He retains God" (he has become a receptacle in which God can be received and retained). Ultimately, the name "Israel" became more than just his new identity; it became the signature of the nation that would issue out from him.

The point is that Jacob was so desperate for God's will that he was willing to wrestle with this heavenly being who had the power to flick him into outer space. Perhaps he sensed that God cannot resist a hungry warrior who will do whatever it takes to get more of the Spirit.

## WHATEVER IT TAKES

Apparently, God loves it when we aren't satisfied with what he's already done, but we are still craving more. We just can't get enough of God's presence. All that matters to us is that he is pleased with us. We could relax and take a break from spirituality by staying in bed the extra hour—or two or three—but instead we lift our head from the fluffy pillows, crawl out from beneath the comfortable covers, sleepily stagger into the prayer closet of our home (wherever that may be), and say, "Not my will but thine be done." We are hungry!

When everyone around you is enjoying the birthday party or the Christmas banquet with all the delicacies that are making your stomach rumble, and you look into the face of temptation and say, "No thank you, I will wait on the Lord," you, my friend, want it badly enough. You are on your way to receiving something far more delicious in the end: an answer or a miracle or a ministry from God that will far outweigh whatever is being served in front of you that night.

## PAIN YOU WON'T REMEMBER

Someone is hungry for more. Someone is willing to suffer for it. Someone has a soldier's mentality, and their environment is not going to distract them from their mission. The warrior will suffer physically, emotionally, mentally, financially, verbally, domestically, and even spiritually if his or her assignment requires it. If God has asked a hungry warrior to fast a certain number of days or pray a certain number of hours, you won't be able to stop him or her from completing the mission. The reward at the end of the battle overrides by far the suffering during the fray.

My wife birthed our two sons, Jude and Jhett, seventeen months apart. I remember how nauseous and fatigued and miserable she was for the duration of both pregnancies. She often asked, "What was I thinking? Why am I doing this to myself?" On top of that, I learned from being with her in the delivery room that birthing the babies was harder than all the months carrying those little guys. It's amazing what women go through to give life to a child!

And yet, after Jude was born, my wife remembered none of those hours, days, weeks, and months of pregnancy. After a very hard delivery she was ready for another child a few months later. Why? Because the reward of seeing and hearing the sweet cries of her newborn angel removed the suffering she had endured to get to that moment. The best thing is she gets to enjoy the miracle not just for a moment, but, should the Lord tarry and have favor on us, for decades and decades. In other words, you don't consider the price tag to be all that expensive when you see the value of the blessing you'll be acquiring.

## IT'S TIME TO GO GET IT!

We are living in a generation that doesn't want it. Sadly, there are preachers out there who would run over anyone to have a big preaching engagement, but those same preachers roll over and continue snoring when the Spirit whispers in their ear to wake up and have an encounter with God in prayer. Why? Because there are no audiences in the living room at 4:00 a.m. There's a price to pay for the real thing, but, oh, how real that thing is! I will say it until I die: If you don't want it badly enough to go after it, someone else will. The person who isn't interested in paying the price will be a bystander as the hungry warrior engages in battle inside the arena.

Jesus commanded us to take up our cross and follow him. Most view the cross as simply a burden or a heaviness, but the cross was the cruelest, most painful of all forms of execution in first-century Roman society. Flogging or other forms of inflicting pain usually took place before the crucifixion, then the criminal would be forced to carry his own crossbeam to the place of execution. Many of the elite who expected to be convicted often committed suicide (which was not an option for non-citizens) because the punishment of crucifixion was just too painful to endure. Yet Jesus told his disciples to take up their cross and follow him. Why? Because if you and I aren't willing to go all the way, we won't make it all the way.

Be a warrior; go all out; never stop reaching. How long? "Till death do you part." Nothing is allowed to dissuade the warrior who is starving for more of the presence of the Lord. As for me, I would rather die than eat when I'm on a good long fast. There's no food out there, as delicious as it might be, that can satisfy my spiritual tastebuds when I'm hungry for the supernatural.

## EDEN'S APPLES

If you need further convincing, ask your oldest ancestors, Adam and Eve. Talk about the perfect life! No earthly place could compare to Eden, the garden designed and planted by Almighty God. Any botanist or landscape artist who saw this garden would have dropped their jaw in disbelief. Adam and Eve were privileged to hear the audible voice of their creator as he came each day to walk with them in the garden. Yet there was one irresistible attraction that ruined all of this perfection and tranquility. What was it? Food. This food wasn't even chocolate; it was just fruit. Fruit is good, but in my opinion, it pales in comparison to anything with chocolate chips in it!

Satan knew if Adam and Eve disobeyed and ate the fruit, their eyes would be opened and they would become like God, knowing both good and evil. How did he know? He was right there listening to God's instructions about not eating the fruit of the tree of the knowledge of good and evil. This told him the way to mankind's downfall was through his stomach. Sure enough, Adam and Eve couldn't refrain from the one thing they were commanded not to eat. They threw away the most intimate connection with deity for the tantalizing taste of a piece of fruit.

Don't let that serpent entwine itself around your shoulder and whisper into your spirit that you can have all of God without saying no to the plate that's loaded with all of your favorites. Food fills the stomach, but fasting fills the soul and feeds the spirit. I don't recommend going into battle against a person who fasts often. I've seen some bitter people go against the fast-er and they never come out on top.

When you're under attack, nothing prompts God to act on your behalf like fasting and praying. Fasting is the soul declaring, "Not my will but thine be done." As hard as it may be to not defend yourself, try fasting first and see what happens when God defends you. Oh, how hell hates this war tactic! Demons know when you get into that mindset, that kind of desperation, that type of hunger that means it is only a matter of time before God shows up on your behalf. Hell may tempt you to stop fasting, but that means hell is afraid of what you're doing.

## FOCUS, YOUNG PROPHET

In 1 Kings 13 there's an account of a young prophet from Judah whom God called to Bethel in Israel to prophesy against the golden-calf altar King Jeroboam had set up. His message was gruesome: "Oh, altar, altar! This is what the Lord says: A child named Josiah will be born into the dynasty of David. On you he will sacrifice the priests on the pagan shrines who come here to burn incense, and human bones will be burned on you. . . . The Lord has promised to give this sign: This altar will be split apart and its ashes will be poured out on the ground" (1 Kings 13:2–3, NLT).

Enraged by this prophecy, King Jeroboam pointed at the young prophet and shouted, "Seize that man!" Instantly, the king's hand and arm withered. Then a wide crack opened up in the altar and ashes poured out. Fear struck the heart of the king, and he begged the young prophet, "Please ask the Lord your God to restore my hand again!" So the man of God prayed and the king's hand was restored. Jeroboam obviously was a little in awe, for he invited the young man to the palace for a meal and promised to give him a gift. The young man refused, however, explaining that God had told him not to eat or drink anything in Israel, and that he should go home a different way than he had come.

The young man turned and left. Along the journey he must have grown weary because we next see him resting in the shade of a tree. An elder prophet rides up on a donkey and asks if he is the young prophet who testified against the altar. He coaxes, "You must be tired and hungry. Why don't you come home with me and have a meal?"

The young prophet explains the Lord's mandate, but the old prophet lies and says, "But the Lord told me to bring you back to my house to have something to eat and drink!" The young prophet heedlessly abandons his fast and fills his belly with the old man's bread and water. Even as the food is in his mouth, the old man turns on him and prophesies, "You have defied the word of the Lord and have disobeyed the command the Lord your God gave you. Because of this, your body will not be buried in the grave of your ancestors." (See 1 Kings 13:13:21–22, NLT.) The old prophet saddles his donkey, gives it to the young prophet, and sends him on his way. Sure enough, the young man hasn't gone far before a lion meets him in the way and kills him, leaving the body lying in the road with the donkey and the lion standing next to it.

This story serves to illustrate hell's interest in fasting. The devil believes in the efficacy of obedience and prayer and fasting. He has to believe because he can't deny the devastating effects on his evil kingdom of a man or woman who obeys and prays and fasts.

## WELCOME TO SPIRITUAL WARFARE

One of the greatest biblical cases one can study to find inspiration to attack the kingdom of darkness is found in Daniel 10. For twenty-one days Daniel had eaten no choice food (delicacies);

no meat or wine had entered his mouth. This intensity drew the spirit world's attention on both sides. That's what fasting does: it activates spiritual warfare.

After twenty-one days Daniel was visited by an angel of the Lord, who declared that his prayer had been heard on the first day of his fast. However, the answer was delayed by the prince of Persia, a high-ranking evil spirit with authority over an entire nation to stop one man on a fast from getting an answer. But God sent his angel some help: Michael the archangel, the angel of war!

Welcome to warfare in the spiritual realm. Angels and demons aren't fairies with feathers; they are created spirit-beings in the heavens who fight against each other for your future. Thankfully, heaven will not stand idly by when a warrior continues fasting for a breakthrough. God will send help!

When the angel finally got through to Daniel, he told him that he and the angel Michael were on their way to fight the combined forces of the prince of Persia and the prince of Grecia (Greece). Demonic spirits apparently have assignments over nations, regions, counties, and cities. In order for hell to stop Daniel's prayer from getting through, these demonic overlords had to abandon their posts. In other words, Satan was more worried about one man on a fast than he was about an entire nation of people. What a compliment!

In the end, Daniel received his breakthrough. Someone reading this right now is feeling the drawing of the Spirit to go on a fast. But you're also hearing the threats of the enemy. Hell is worried that you—the average, kind-hearted, nice guy or girl, that good Christian who isn't really a threat to the opposing forces—are about to become a hungry warrior.

The question I have for you is, are you willing to go for it? Why not? It's time to step up and get involved in the battle. Make hell fear every time you get out of bed in the middle of the night to pray. Cause the dark side to worry that you're going to say "No food tomorrow" because you need a warrior angel to get the answer through. When your feet hit the floor tomorrow, that battle is on. Go, soldier! Want it badly enough to go get it!

## CHAPTER 3

# Spiritual Authority

Some people reading this chapter may think I'm crazy or delusional. Others will ponder the contents as Mary did the angel's message about the pregnancy she was entering. Yet others will eat this chapter like it is their last meal on death row; they realize the necessity of grasping and attaining spiritual authority.

First of all, spiritual authority means having power or dominion in the spirit. It deals with spirits, not flesh. As Jesus informed Nicodemus, "That which is born of the flesh is flesh; and that which is born of the Spirit is spirit" (John 3:6).

Notice in the latter phrase of the verse that the first mention of "Spirit" is capitalized and the second mention is not. This is because the first word signifies the Spirit of God and the second refers to the human spirit. You cannot have spiritual authority without having God's Spirit. He is the King of kings, Lord of lords, and Spirit of spirits. Jesus told Nicodemus, "You must be born of the Spirit."

There must be a day or night when a spiritual birthing takes place for you to even enter the spirit world. If you want to know how to do this, I encourage you to read the first eight verses of John 3 and then reference Acts 2, 10, and 19 for demonstrations of how people—just like you and me—were born of the Spirit.

You will find that when someone receives the Holy Spirit there is physical evidence that comes along with the spiritual impartation. The person born of the Spirit will speak in other tongues. What does that mean? If your native tongue is English, when you are filled with the Spirit (or born of the Spirit), you will speak in a language you do not understand as English. You will have no idea what you are speaking, but at the same time you will know that the words coming out of you aren't you at all, but rather the Spirit of the Lord speaking through you.

> *He that believeth on me, as the scripture hath said, out of his belly shall flow rivers of living water. (But this spake he of the Spirit, which they that believe on him should receive: for the Holy Ghost was not yet given; because that Jesus was not yet glorified.)* (John 7:38–39)

This is how the Spirit of God gives a person spiritual birth. The Greek word "born" is gennao, meaning to be born or begotten, to come forth. We all at one point were born in the flesh. We left the darkness of the womb and came forth into the light. It happens the same way spiritually. To be born of the Spirit means the Spirit births your spirit. You are born again.

The Spirit of God living inside of someone is a nightmare to the forces of hell. The reason for this torment on the demonic side is that there is no greater power or authority than the Spirit of God. Which leads us into the next dimension of understanding the spirit world.

## THE SPIRIT OF GOD REIGNS SUPREME

There are four distinct elements of the spirit world that are active in the physical world you and I live in. The first and supreme authority in both the spirit world and the natural world is, of course, the Spirit of God. As discussed previously, no other spirit compares to his Spirit. In creation it was the Spirit of the Lord that moved on the waters before he opened up his mouth and commanded, "Let there be light!" Those words shot out of his mouth at 186,000 miles per second and have not stopped soaring at that speed since!

The Spirit of the Lord has no opposition, no adversary, no challenger, no threat, and no other gods to deal with. For there to be another god, the Lord would have to make this deity, and therefore because He created it, it would be a creation that would be subservient to its creator.

If the Spirit of the Lord moves on you, you will not be able to remain depressed, discouraged, or in doubt. He is light, and all darkness flees from his presence. His presence dominates, dictates, and determines the very existence of the heavens and the earth's atmosphere. The reason you must understand this is because true spiritual authority begins with the One who has all authority— the Lord Jesus Christ. Before individuals can walk in true authority in the spirit world, they must have within them the One with all authority and dominion. No one can claim to have spiritual authority if they don't have his Spirit living inside of them.

## ANGELIC SPIRITS

The second dimension in the spirit world is the dimension of angels. Angels are on a higher creative order than mankind. I disagree with people who say humans can command angels, because that claim is unbiblical. Man was made a little lower than the angels and nowhere in the Bible do you find people commanding God's heavenly host. Flesh cannot command spirit.

Holy angels are ministering spirits that work for God. They have no fleshly will, for they are not made of flesh as you and I are but they are completely composed of spirit. According to the Bible, God sometimes commands angels to appear as humans to deliver messages, to help, to defend, or to test human individuals.

> *Be not forgetful to entertain strangers: for thereby some have entertained angels unawares."* (Heb. 13:2)

This verse indicates that not every stranger you see is a person. God had to become human to get our attention and save us, so it makes sense that sometimes when he speaks to us or tests us that he would use a similar formula and send an angel down in the form of a person. Why would he do this? If an angel appeared to you sporting enormous wings covered in white feathers, with a golden breastplate, and a glowing halo to test you by saying, "Treat this person you're about to meet with love and kindness," you would say, "Yes, absolutely!" Meanwhile, you would be trying to calm your thundering heartbeats because you have just seen an angel. Instead, the angel comes to you as a stranger to see how you will act—or react to them—without the "spiritual" intervention.

Another thing angels are sent to do is guard God's children. I believe if you fear the Lord, an angel is always near you.

> *The angel of the Lord encampeth round about them that fear him, and delivereth them.* (Ps. 34:7)

The Hebrew word "encampeth" is chanah, meaning to decline, incline, bend down, cover as a tent. In other words, if you're a God-fearer, no matter from what angle the enemy comes at you, the angel will bend down and encircle you to hide you from the attack and quench the fiery darts or other weapons hurled by hell. It pays to fear the Lord!

The next time Satan tries to threaten you, don't fear him; fear the Lord. You will be thankful you did. If you fear anything more than you fear the Lord, that thing is your lord. If I can convince you that fearing God above all is the secret to winning any spiritual battle that involves you being threatened, then I have handed you a weapon that hell greatly fears.

The greatest assignment angels carry out on a daily basis is, in my opinion, the carrying of prayers from earth to heaven to pour out before the Lord. Daniel 10 and Revelation 5 and 8 validate this statement. Angels carry your prayers to the throne room in a vial or censer and pour them out before the Lord. I could fill pages and pages on this subject, but I'll try to be as brief as possible.

When a saint of God begins to pray, an angel is sent to pick up the prayer and usher it into the presence of the Lord. Daniel heard those words from the angel after he had prayed for twenty-one days. The angel told him, "I am come for thy words" (Dan. 10:12). But just as angels are sent to take the prayers up, demonic forces are sent to prevent this from happening. Who wins? You are the deciding factor. The more you fast and pray about something the more likely the answer will come.

Regardless of what others might say, the time of day that you pray is important. I've heard it all: "It doesn't matter what time you pray. God hears you the same at 4:00 p.m. as he does at 4:00 a.m." This is true, but let me bring up some points to consider. First, Jacob wrestled with the angel until daybreak. The reason the angel asked to leave was because it was time for him to ascend. He was ready to take the prayers up. If angels are coming and going at daybreak, it behooves us to be up before daybreak with our repentance done and being deeply involved in supplication or intercession.

Second, the reason I feel early-morning prayer is more valuable (i.e., if you have a normal work schedule—I understand some have the graveyard shift) is because it is much more of a sacrifice to climb out of the king-size bed at 4:00 or 5:00 in the morning to go meet your God than it is at 4:00 or 5:00 in the afternoon when you are wide awake. Let me clarify that I pray at night also, but I find the deeper things of the Spirit usually come when there is a sacrifice on my part to get to the meeting place with the Savior.

I believe we all need to pray morning, noon, and night. Daily prayer should be our top priority. I'm not condemning you if you'd rather pray at noon than at 5:00 in the morning. The truth be told, we should all try to be a little more like Daniel, who had multiple prayer meetings each day. I simply know that if I need an answer, I go early to the throne. I have seen more prayers answered on the same day I prayed them by rising early to pray than I ever could dream of just praying when I get around to it during my busy day.

I believe it shows the Lord our desperation and desire for an answer when we leave comfort and step into consecration. Sacrificial prayer is powerful. In my experience, the days I pray early go far better than the days where I'm searching for a prayer slot in my crazy schedule. I'm less stressed, worried, and frustrated when I know I've already put every conversation, encounter, meeting, car ride, flight, situation, dilemma, and need into God's hands before I did anything else that day. The opposite is also true: when I don't put these things into his omniscient care early, I can expect stress, anxiety, frustration, and any other discouraging words that could fill in the blanks for that day.

So, needless to say, angels are attracted to prayer. Angels are dispatched daily with specific missions. Some are sent to protect, some are sent to speak, and some are sent to gather prayers. Some angels are sent to heal; some are sent to destroy. The Bible records God visiting the Egyptians and smiting their firstborn sons the night before the miraculous deliverance of the Israelites. The deed was done by an angel of death sent by God.

I believe a person is much more likely to have an encounter with an angel if he or she is near where the angel is sent to work that day. Whether or not the person even recognizes they are near an angel is up to the Lord allowing their eyes to be opened and their understanding to be enlightened. Angels work for the Lord just as most of us do, except they don't have the flesh barrier we must deal with on a daily basis. But we have a privilege angels can only desire: although we are flesh, we have access to God's Spirit living in us!

## THE DEMONIC SPIRIT

The third dimension of the spirit world is the demonic dimension. To understand this dimension, we must look into Satan's past. Most Bible readers know that Satan once was known as Lucifer, the angel of light. Ezekiel 28 records in great detail the intricate characteristics of the king of Tyrus, also known as Lucifer.

The first thing that jumps off the page is that God endued Lucifer with wisdom; apparently, he was the wisest angel ever created. People who call the devil dumb or ignorant are revealing their own spiritual ignorance. We certainly don't glorify his wisdom, for it is corrupt, polluted, perverted, and purely evil. That being said, we understand that before his eviction from the heavenly host, Lucifer was very wise. He now uses this wisdom against human beings.

If you've never smoked a cigarette, you probably won't have a drug dealer at your door today offering you cocaine. That attempt of hell would fail miserably because you wouldn't even be tempted to try the drug. If you've never tasted alcohol, you probably won't be tempted to stop by the liquor store after work to waste your paycheck on spirits. Temptations like these will fall like a lead balloon because they come to you in an area of strength.

Satan is wily. When a demonic spirit comes against you, it comes in the weak places—places where you have fallen frequently. For instance, if you struggle with an addiction, until you prove consistently to the forces of darkness that you've locked that door both externally and internally, you can expect that temptation to appear again and again in your life, usually when you're alone.

The greatest ways to lock the door to these persistent temptations and failures are prayer and fasting. Asking God for strength and authority is a wonderful way to get started, then turn up the heat by laying your flesh on that altar through a good fast. Once this has been accomplished, another way to keep the door locked is to choose a day out of every week and set it aside for fasting. This will keep your flesh on the altar, and when those evil spirits come knocking, they will find the door is locked and will go away in Jesus' name.

Fasting kills the flesh and sends a thunderous message into the ranks of hell that you're not what you used to be and you will be victorious when this blood bath of a war ends. The Roman theologian Tertullian once said, "Fasting, if practiced with the right intention, makes man a friend of God, the demons are aware of that." How amazing to know, as a child of God, that hell is scared to death when you go on a fast!

## THE HUMAN SPIRIT

The fourth and final dimension is the human dimension. The reason it is the lowest dimension is because, according to the Bible, God made us lower than angels. If the human spirit were enough to thwart off opposing spiritual forces, there would be no need for Calvary or angels to keep charge over us.

Our human spirit has "antennae" that can sense things without a word being said. For instance, you can walk into a room and immediately feel if someone doesn't like you, even though they've never met you before. The opposite is also true: you can walk into a room and see someone you've never met but you can feel a connection with them as if you've been friends for a long time. This is one of the many ways human spirits communicate.

Your human spirit is sensitive to the spirit world as well. The fleshly part of you is clueless sometimes, but your human spirit will sense things. This is why the Holy Ghost inside someone is so dynamic. When someone's human spirit is filled with the Holy Spirit, they are guided and given clarity in all of life's situations.

For example, a person without the Holy Spirit may walk into an atmosphere full of worldly people and sense something isn't right. Their human spirit doesn't connect with the vibe they're receiving. They're troubled, but they can't quite put their finger on the reason. They just know that they feel uncomfortable and would rather not be there. In contrast, a person full of the Holy Ghost feels the same emotion when they step into that atmosphere, but they can sense if there are demons in the room, or someone is possessed, or something bad is about to happen. Why?

Because the Holy Ghost inside of them is the Lord of glory, and nothing gets by him.

Whether either of these two people stays in the room depends on the will of their human spirit. If the person without the Holy Ghost ignores that inner frustration, they'll stay. If the person with the Holy Ghost ignores the whisper of the Almighty, they'll also stay, and, I might add, regret it later.

Whispers from the Lord in your ear are like sonic booms in the spirit world. When the supreme spiritual authority speaks to someone, there is no greater communication on the planet. If you truly desire to have spiritual authority, you must pursue God's Spirit. The way to do this is through prayer and fasting. Fasting gives a microphone to that whisper from the Lord; it amplifies his voice until you can hear it loud and clear.

## CHAPTER 4

# Preparing for a Fast

Individuals who are planning to fast must first prepare themselves in multiple areas of their lives, especially if they have a long fast in mind. By "long fast," I mean anything beyond three days—but especially if the plan is to fast seven or more days. There are several factors to consider when it is time to fast: spiritual factors, physical factors, emotional factors, mental factors, schedule factors, financial factors, and even family factors will be involved at some point or at multiple times during that period of consecration.

Let us begin with the spiritual factor. How does one prepare spiritually for a spiritual journey? First, I can tell you that the desire to fast is usually born of spiritual unction. I realize some individuals fast for physical reasons, but the average child of God who feels called to fast is being moved on by the Spirit. The desire to fast is the invasion of one's flesh by the Spirit of the Lord.

Preparing spiritually for a fast often gets overlooked and ne-glected, then people wonder why they fail to finish the number of days they had planned to fast. People will always fast longer if they've been consecrating themselves for a significant span of time before the fast begins. If people expect to last for the duration of the fast without leading up to it by prayer and intimacy with God, the flesh that was never crucified is still very much alive and will rise up to abort their fasting plans.

We see fasting as crucifying the flesh, and it does to an extent. But please ponder this: In the Old Testament when they brought the sacrificial animal to the altar, they killed it before burning it on the altar. We need to take the same approach to our upcoming fast; we need to sacrifice our flesh before we fast. We need to prepare spiritually, not just physically.

How do we prepare spiritually to fast? How do we kill the flesh before we burn it in the fire of fasting? The answer might be different for each individual, but let me give an example that might connect with many who are reading this. Fasting turns down the volume of the world so you can hear the voice of the Spirit. What if you were to disconnect from social media or from staring at your phone screen for a few weeks before you begin the fast? I imagine you would hear from God much sooner during your fast. I imagine your answers would come quicker than you expect because you showed up at the altar of fasting with dead flesh ready to be burned.

Too many times, we offer the Lord flesh that is still alive. We want to put our flesh on the altar for a while and then let it off once it has lain there long enough to satisfy our conscience. May the new cry of our heart become, "Let it die! Let it burn! Not my will but thine be done, Lord."

The angel told Daniel after twenty-one days of consecration that his need had been heard on the first day. Why? Because Daniel had a habit of opening his window three times a day for prayer. How many "windows" are open on your phone right now at this moment? How many windows have you opened in the Spirit today with prayer? I firmly believe that disconnecting from the world before a fast will lead to greater spiritual encounters during the fast.

In Exodus 34, God told Moses not to let anyone on or near the mountain that he was about to climb while fasting. God didn't want any competing voices to interfere during Moses' heavenly encounter. It is dangerous for us to try to approach God in order to hear his voice while, at the same time, doubting he will speak, so we bring other voices along to fill in the silence.

Consistent consecration is compared, in my mind, to a physical bootcamp a soldier must pass to be eligible to enter the battle. Soldiers must prove themselves daily at the same times, passing the same drills, enduring the same pressures, and strengthening the same muscles before they can even think about being deployed on active duty to defend their nation.

The same goes for the one who is about to enter the war zone that we call fasting. You must prove to the Master that you're prepared in all aspects before he will release you to go into battle. Why? Because fasting not only is a war in your fleshly body but in the spirit world as well. You will enter places you've never seen or heard about, and you'd better be ready for whatever or whoever is out there.

The best way I know how to prepare myself spiritually for a fast is to pray at the same time every day, if possible, along with reading a consistent number of chapters in the Bible each day. I believe in praying for days, weeks, and even months in advance according to the length of the fast you're planning.

The longer the fast the greater the consecration needs to be beforehand. The more you pray about it, the more you will focus on it. The fast will eventually consume you if you have bathed it in daily prayer prior to starting. Don't be afraid to talk to the

Lord about the fast. Details, small or great, matter to God if they matter to you.

You will discover that you will be more motivated when the day of the fast begins because you have been bombarding heaven with prayer meetings and requests that are connected to the time of sacrifice you are about to enter.

## PREPARE TO DETOX

There are physical factors (preparations) that should take place when preparing to start a fast. I've learned this the hard way. According to the number of days you desire to fast, that is the number of days you should prepare your body before beginning the fast. I have done several fasts where I felt to start on a certain day and didn't do anything to prepare physically, and it hurt my body because I didn't remove toxins by making healthier eating choices before starting.

Your body will remove many toxins during the first three to four days of a fast, causing headaches, mood swings, fatigue, and other physical manifestations. If you've been eating junk food that is horrible for you and drinking caffeine drinks, you're going to experience withdrawal symptoms and migraines once the fast begins.

There are three major types of foods you need to cut out of your diet when preparing for a fast: red meats, sugars, and caffeine. For instance, if you're planning to fast seven days, then seven days before your start date tell the steaks, chocolate, and sweet tea goodbye so your body won't flip out on you and make you the grumpiest person on the planet.

If you don't do this, by day two of your fast your body will be craving these "luxuries," and you'll be one miserable human being! Obviously, if you make healthful food choices as a lifestyle, this will greatly diminish the side effects of detoxing at the onset of the fast.

I realize that sometimes the Lord calls us to a fast without much warning. We must obey in those circumstances, but for the most part, we should try to prepare in advance if we see a fast looming on the horizon.

Another physical way to prepare for a fast is exercise. I know this isn't everyone's favorite thing to do, and some would like to but can't. However, exercise has an immense impact on how you feel physically. Exercise causes the body to release several beneficial hormones: serotonin (restful sleep, healthy appetite, more energy, clearer thinking); endorphins (exhilaration); estrogen (burns fat in women); dopamine (the pleasure chemical); and growth factors (stimulates production of muscle tissue). These hormones promote good feelings that trigger positive thoughts and happiness.

Exercise is something I greatly enjoy, even when I'm fasting. It's an incredible outlet for me to disconnect from stress and pressure, whether spiritual or natural. It gives me mental focus and causes me to relax and get my mind off of it all, whatever "it all" may be at the moment.

The next type of preparation for a fast is emotional preparation. You need to be ready emotionally to go without food before attempting a fast; otherwise, stress will weigh you down before you start. This is an exciting time you are about to engage in, therefore worrying yourself to death over little things doesn't help your mindset going into the fast. It will only deplete your drive to complete the fast and damage your confidence that you can do this.

The greatest way to help yourself emotionally is to read the word of God. Reading the Bible brings a peace that passes all understanding. His word is the strength you need to rely on daily; it is your spiritual food. People who say the Bible is boring are spiritual prisoners of war that are starving to death of their own volition. Nothing will make your emotions relax and rejuvenate like the word of the Lord.

*Thou wilt keep him in perfect peace, whose mind is stayed on thee: because he trusteth in thee.* (Isa. 26:3)

Emotions can change on a whim; therefore, the more stable your emotions are during a fast the longer you will be able to endure on that fast. The enemy tries to work through my emotions sometimes. If he can frustrate me in an important task or assignment, then he can distract me and cause me to lose focus on the goal or destiny that is at stake. In other words, if he gets to my emotions, he can cause me to quit a fast before I'm actually released from it by the Lord.

When your emotions get out of control, you often do things that you later regret. You say things, or worse, you act in ways that are out of character for you. Your mismanaged emotions may leave a faulty mental impact on someone else's mind about who you are.

During a fast, your emotions will fly out of normal range, especially if the fast is several days. When certain hormones are released into your system, they send signals to your brain that it's time to eat. You usually obey these orders, but now you're rejecting those signals and refusing to submit to their demands. Your emotions will yell, "That's what you think! I want food!" Prayer will help get these emotions under subjection, allowing you to refocus on the opportunity before you.

The next factor is the mental factor. Successful fasting probably is due just as much to mental readiness as it is to physical readiness. Make no mistake about it; you'd better be ready for war mentally when you enter the fasting world. Your mind will get weak, weary, and worn on a fast, especially if your mind is used to feasting on carnality. Thus it is important that you feed your mind spiritual food while you're withholding food from your physical body.

You will discover that your mind will crave food, pleasure, entertainment, and relaxation during your fast. The only way to take your mind off of these distractions is to feed it with the things that will strengthen and sustain you spiritually. The importance of reading the Bible has already been mentioned, but let me reiterate: nothing will feed your mind the positive thoughts it needs like the scriptures.

> *And be not conformed to this world: but be ye transformed by the renewing of your mind, that ye may prove what is that good, and acceptable, and perfect will of God.* (Rom. 12:2)

## THE CHOICE IS YOURS

You can either conform or be transformed. What you dwell on mentally will determine that choice. You can become what entertains you and simply flow with the current (that is, to conform), or you can be transformed—become who and what you have always dreamed of becoming in God.

Transformation, according to the scriptures, is a result of a renewing of one's mind. The Greek word for "renewing" is anakainosis, meaning to renovate or completely change for the better. The more renovation that takes place in your mind the better things will begin to appear and feel. A renewed mind will cause you to see things differently than you would have seen them had you simply been pulled along by the current. If you renew your mind daily, then you are in a continual process of transformation; you are always changing for the better.

However, if you aren't renewing your mind, then you'll begin to conform to whatever the surrounding environment is, regardless of how negative that may be. Only a daily mental renewal will lead to total transformation in all areas of life.

This renewal must be done through the word of God and through prayer. If you are preparing to go on a fast, renewing your mind daily is a must. Get rid of the depressing clutter and pressing distractions by entertaining the presence of the Lord daily as much as possible. The more of his voice or words that enter into your mind the more renovation takes place, resulting in more transformation.

Daily renewing of the mind is also the avenue to finding the perfect will of God. It clears your spiritual vision for the direction you need for the decision at hand. According Romans 12:2, it is the way to prove what his will is. In other words, you may miss the will of God if your mind is always conforming and never renewing.

Transform the way you think today. Don't let another day go by just existing and hoping for a different outcome than spending the rest of your days in aimless living. Renovate your spiritual house and you will be shocked at the dreams and desires that are still alive that you have boxed away in the closet of your thoughts.

When someone renovates a house, they know it will cost thousands of dollars to transform what they currently see with their eyes into what they can see only in their mind. They have a vision, but fruition of the vision comes with a price tag. Yet they consider it money will spent and inconvenience well worth it; they would rather enjoy the result of the renovation than live in (conform) to the existing state of the house.

## RENOVATION CAN MEAN DEMOLITION

A derelict house won't become a dream-house reality, until the renovators call in a demolition crew. This is because old things have to be demolished before new things can be built. Similarly, a person's old thought patterns and processes must be demolished before transformation can take place. Negative, pessimistic, bitter, envious, and jealous thoughts have to go during the renovation.

If you've already been demolishing thoughts that you know lead to negative words and actions, my friend, you've begun your mental renovation that will result in a much brighter future than had you continued down the path of conformity. Transformation has begun.

Demolition can be painful because you're destroying a pattern that's been ingrained into your thinking process. Some people, during the demolition phase of their house renovation, shed tears because of the memories they've made in that particular area of the house. They feel a sentimental connection to what is being removed, even though they know it has to be done. For instance, an existing wall has become an obstacle to the open concept they know their family needs so they will be comfortable in a larger space. Maybe the wall has held pictures, but now it's just in the way of the future. It's blocking the view. It has to be demolished.

What walls have you let stand too long in your mind? Find them and get out the wrecking ball. It's time for renovation!

One benefit of fasting is that God reveals walls in your nature and life that need to be demolished so renovation can take place. His Spirit is like an inspector that comes into the home and says this or that must be changed before you can attempt to live here. If something in the home is not up to code and therefore can cause you harm in the future, the inspector has the duty to inform you that an immediate change is necessary. The demolition must begin despite how long the flaw has been around. Fasting summons the inspector. Fasting reveals the flaws. On the positive side, fasting moves you to action to secure that area of your life for a better future. Once you have fixed the flaw, you can say the fast was successful.

Some people have walls in their marriage that were built in their childhood, and they subconsciously expect their spouse to operate within those walls because "that's how things are with me." They'd rather not demolish any concepts or ideas that have worked for them in the past than to make peace with the person they are building their future with now. Their tacit message is "That wall worked great in my home as a kid. The concept wasn't debatable in the past, so my spouse needs to understand that I want that wall up. I feel safe with it in place. I don't trust their idea about my future. If my spouse wants the wall to come down, I don't know what I will see on the other side of that wall." This mentality forces the spouse to coexist with concepts and views that are based on insecurity or just plain old pride. Fasting will challenge you to become more understanding to your spouse. It will make you a better listener. It will open your eyes to the fact that the concept you think is a must might just be a wall that was a must for your parents.

It is a given that we all should be trying to move our families closer to God. To that end, there are some things you just can't compromise no matter who your spouse is. Some things are not walls; they are spiritual foundations that made you the man or woman you have become. But if your foundation is cracked, fasting will open your eyes to what needs to be fortified and strengthened in your life and what simply needs to come down. It's demolition time!

## BECOME THE FAST

We have established that mental preparation before a fast is necessary for the fast to last. That is, you need to eat, sleep, think, and become the fast. Talk with your pastor about the fast you're planning to attempt. Think about it so much that it's the first thing besides Jesus that you think of in the morning and the last thing besides Jesus that crosses your mind before you go to sleep.

When preparing for a long fast, I try to suffuse my mind with thoughts of fasting. I read everything I can on fasting. I pray about it. I think about it in the morning. I engulf myself with it so I won't be easily discouraged after my fast has begun. Why? Once discouragement settles on an individual who is fasting, the fast will come to a rapid end. This is why mental preparation is huge. The longer and harder you train mentally for a fast, the stronger you will be mentally for that war.

## MENTAL TOUGHNESS

There is something about people who are tough mentally that gives them an edge over their enemies. People can be in excruciating physical pain to the degree of fearing for their life, but because they are so mentally strong they endure and refuse to give up.

They have learned that mental strength triumphs over physical suffering.

The apostle Paul, when describing to King Agrippa several afflictions he had personally endured for Jesus' sake, said, "I think myself happy" (Acts 26:2). In other words, you can say, "It doesn't matter what I have to suffer. In my mind I've already pinned hell to the mat. The battle is over. No matter what I go through, I have mental toughness that makes me happy no matter what." If you can find that place, you will win the war every time.

Mental toughness is vital to the fast-er because the thoughts are going to come that whisper "Give up" or "This isn't worth the struggle because nothing will change after this sacrifice." Mark these words down: When thoughts like these invade, there had better be power in your mind that rebukes them and says, "I will press on," or the fast will be over and you will be wondering what could have and should have happened.

## MAKE UP YOUR MIND

True soldiers will never quit in battle; they would rather die first. Are there times when every fiber of your being is yelling, "Stop! You can't go on anymore!" Sure. But the reason you don't quit is you have learned the value of mental toughness. What you are suffering and enduring physically does not compare to what you are convinced of mentally. You have made up your mind. A made-up mind in a soldier of the cross who is fasting is a nightmare to the demons of hell.

I was several days into a fast when everyone wanted to eat at The Cheesecake Factory, and I had to go with them. Did the food look good? Yes! Was I hungry? Absolutely! Did my flesh think about stopping the fast to indulge in some Oreo cheesecake? As soon as we got there! Was I actually ever close to breaking the fast? Not a chance! I had come too far to throw away a future of fresh anointing to enjoy the taste of cheesecake in my mouth. You must endure some things before you can enjoy other things. When your mind is focused, you have an advantage and you know it. I would venture to say that if you enter a lengthy fast without that mental edge in your spirit, you will not last more than a couple days.

Before I embark on a lengthy fast, I spend more time mentally preparing than anything else. I've learned through the years that the greatest battles during a fast aren't always encounters with demons (keep reading and you'll see what I mean), but several times the toughest battle during the fast will be a desire for Italian food or whatever type of food is your favorite. In other words, the flesh can really put up a fight. What you dwell on mentally will become what you desire, talk about, and even pursue once the fast is over.

## SCHEDULING YOUR FAST

When preparing to go on an extended fast, it is wise to consult your calendar. Obviously, if the Lord tells you to start the fast immediately, you obey his voice and work your schedule around it. But if God hasn't told you to start fasting on a certain date, I recommend looking at your schedule and trying to fast when there's a little downtime. You may be thinking that you have absolutely no downtime so this doesn't matter, but look again just in case.

At the very least, you can start the fast on a day when you know your mind will be focused and engaged with what you're feeling called to do. Again, the more focused you are, the longer you will last. Give yourself an edge and begin when you know you will most likely not be distracted. I usually start my fasts on a Sunday night around midnight and then enter the week on the fast. The reason for this is Mondays are normally either my traveling days or recovering days after preaching on Sundays, so it is usually when I have the most time to think. I prefer to start extended fasts at midnight—but I admit I can be OCD at times.

Another reason why scheduling your fast is important is because when you plan something and put it on the calendar, you are more likely to follow through with it than to just start whenever. If it's in your datebook or on your iPhone, then you'll probably think about it more often as the day approaches than to just start whenever it comes to mind.

If you have a week that is crammed with travel, appointments, meetings, deadlines, stress, speaking engagements, physical labor, or fill-in-the-blank, and then the next week after that you have a couple days off, you might use some wisdom and consider beginning the fast then.

I will caution you that sometimes unscheduled things will pop up unexpectedly when you're on a longer fast and you'll have to adjust on the fly. For example, in 2013 I went on a forty-day fast and had planned my schedule around it. I'm an ordained evangelist, so traveling and preaching every week is what I do. I thought I had the perfect forty days lined up because all that was on my calendar was preaching on Sundays in places in the vicinity of where we lived in Florida. I had no clue that wild revival fires would break out and I would end up preaching twenty times in the forty days, as well as traveling hundreds of miles each week. All I can say is thank the Lord for his supernatural strength and wisdom. I'm glad Jesus knows when I'll be busy and plans accordingly by supplying me with extra strength for the journey. His thoughts have always been higher than mine.

## FASTING WILL MAKE YOU REST

At times I have planned extended fasts while looking at the calendar and was grateful I did because I've learned to appreciate the rest that comes when I fast. If you never rest, fast for a little bit. (I'm grinning sheepishly as I write this.) The hands on the clock that usually race like rabbits through each day will slow to a snail's pace during a fast. Seven days will feel like thirty days. This is due to the fact that we typically spend anywhere between two and four hours a day preparing and eating food. The clock now says, "Hello. There's nothing for you to do right now since you aren't eating. I suggest twiddling your thumbs to keep you from going stir crazy." You must find things to do to fill up that time where you would normally be cooking and eating. Obviously, the most advantageous activity during these moments is to feed yourself spiritually through the word of God and prayer. Meditation on his word also is excellent, as is reading a spiritual book or listening to preaching. Being alone with God is crucial during a fast.

However, there will be times when you won't feel like praying or plowing through nineteen chapters in Ezekiel. These moments of agony (because that is what they are) should be spent resting. I strongly recommend getting as much sleep as you can during these times. You aren't sinning when you're resting; in fact, you're preparing spiritually for the next wave of warfare or visitation that is coming to your weak and exhausted mind, soul, and body. Some people feel guilty, like they're disobeying God if they ever rest. These are the people who frequently experience burnout.

## THE POSITION OF SPIRITUAL REST

Spiritual rest is just as holy as your prayer time. Some of you reading that sentence disagree with me, because you feel that relaxation is carnal. But please notice I said "spiritual rest." There's a difference in spiritual rest and carnal relaxation.

Carnal relaxation usually involves entertainment that helps you unwind, whereas spiritual rest involves dwelling on the Lord as you regain virtue. Carnal relaxation may temporarily take away stress, but it may make you miss your early morning encounter with God by staying up too late the night before. Spiritual rest will cause the worries to flee, and when you arise, you will wake up hungry and excited to meet the master in the cool of the day.

Needless to say, the more spiritual rest you can attain while fasting the better the fast is going to go for you. I have had incredible revelations, answers, wisdom, and direction come to me while engaging in spiritual rest. Spiritual rest positions your mind to hear from God.

If you need a miracle, word, answer, or direction, I strongly challenge you to position your mind toward the things of God. His voice is so much clearer to the spiritual ear than it is to the carnal ear. Resting in his Spirit will cause you to be more sensitive to his voice and more discerning about listening to voices other than his. This could lead you farther down the path to understanding the spirit world. Let me briefly summarize: If you want to be more sensitive to the Spirit of God and the spirit world in general, then you need to pray every day for discernment and perception, because many voices are out there. Remember Satan can transform himself into an angel of light.

Spiritual discernment is vital. You need to be able to recognize God's voice, your own spirit's voice, and hell's voice. When you face a major decision in your life, these three voices will talk, sometimes all at once. If you are rested spiritually, you will be able to discern the difference in each voice. If you are not rested spiritually but rather have engaged in carnal relaxation at every opportunity, you might miss the right voice.

## CAN THE SPIRIT REST ON YOU?

The word "rest" appears 265 times in the Bible. The first appearance is when Noah let the dove out of the ark. (A dove is a representation of the Holy Spirit, as in when the Spirit of God descended like a dove on Jesus Christ.) Noah's dove found no place to rest (Gen. 8:9). This was a type and shadow of the Spirit looking for a place to rest and not finding one. No human being outside of the ark survived the flood; therefore, there were no shoulders for the dove to land on. The writer of Hebrews offers an example of how vital spiritual rest must become to the believer.

> *There remaineth therefore a rest to the people of God. For he that is entered into his rest, he also hath ceased from his own works, as God did from his. Let us labour therefore to enter into that rest, lest any man fall after the same example of unbelief.* (Heb. 4:9–11)

This passage is loaded with revelation. The word "rest" in the first sentence of this text is the Greek word sabbatismos, meaning to keep the sabbath. Sabbatismos alluded to the physical rest from wandering the ancient Hebrews received when they entered the Promised Land under Joshua. However, Joshua and the twelve tribes did not receive the everlasting rest promised to the children of God.

The Greek word for "rest" in the second sentence of the text is katapausis, meaning "to make to cease; the act of resting, ceasing from labor, or the place of rest, dwelling, fixed abode" (The Complete Word Study Dictionary New Testament). In Psalm 132:4–16, God is represented as searching through the earth for a habitation, and he chooses Zion, saying, "This is my rest for ever: here will I dwell; for I have desired it (Ps. 132:14). The Hebrew word for "rest" from Psalm 132:14 is manuchah, meaning an abode, a place of comfort, ease, quiet, and rest. God has promised an eternal rest in his heavenly abode for believers in Christ after their toils and trials of life on earth are ended. They will cease from their works as God ceased from his. This is referring to the seventh day of creation (Gen. 1) when God's Spirit rested.

In short, we, as the people of God, have a period of rest known as the sabbath (Heb. 4:9). We can spend this time carnally or spiritually. If we spend it carnally, it remains a sabbatismos, or the traditional sabbath day. But if we enter into that spiritual rest mentioned in verse 10, our period of rest becomes a katapausis, wherein we enter that place of quiet, comfort, calm, and rest where God dwells. We decide what our downtime becomes. It can be a routine of relaxation, or it can be a place where God calms the storms, a place of promise that once these trials come to an end, we will feel his blessed presence.

Verse 11 adds that we need to labor to enter into that rest. The Greek word for labor is spoudazo, meaning to hasten or to exert oneself. In other words, do whatever you have to do to enter into that dimension where the Master calms the storm. Is there anything that requires more exertion than fasting? Fasting releases spiritual rest into your life.

## FINANCIAL FACTORS

Another thing to think about when preparing for a fast is your financial situation. If you're like me, you have a budget. Budgeting may seem tedious to some, but even the richest people in the world will tell you that sticking to a weekly budget is a good thing. If you are planning to juice while you fast, you might find that juicing is quite expensive. Your juicer uses up all those vegetables and fruits rather quickly, requiring yet another trip to the produce department.

If you are going to drink water only on an extended fast, you can take advantage of the money you would be spending on food during that time and use it in another area of need in your life, or you could help someone else with their needs. Isaiah 58 mentions giving our bread to the hungry and bringing the poor into our houses when we're fasting.

Fasting can clear the mind and cause you to get your finances in order if they aren't at the moment. There is something about fasting that motivates an individual to clean up any clutter in their life. When fasting, they want everything to be clean around them in their home; the more they fast, the more uncleanness will bother them. Fasting brings order, clarity, and organization into your world.

## THE FAMILY FACTOR

The reason I want to discuss the family factor is because your fast will affect your family members as well, especially if the fast is going to be lengthy. Unless you are planning on being completely isolated from them, the other family members are going to have to live with you when you are weak, grumpy, tired, excited, out of it, light headed, or exhausted. They won't feel the headache from hell that is storming your brain on day three during the process of acidosis (the result of failing to detox prior to starting the fast), but they will definitely be able to tell you aren't feeling well.

If you are married, the more you can discuss the fast with your spouse beforehand the better. I am a big believer in being on the same page with your spouse on these things. Your spouse might not be fasting with you, but he or she has to live with you—and you know how you get when you get hungry. Ask him or her to pray for you and try to understand this is a temporary time of consecration to the Lord; therefore, you may not be yourself every moment of the day.

If you are not married but living at home with family, try to act like a Christian. If you feel they don't need to know you are fasting, then you have a responsibility to be extra kind. If you aren't, they will know something is going on. Jesus said to wash your face and act like everything is normal.

Sometimes family members can sway the outcome of a fast if the person fasting is closely connected to them. This can be either positive or negative, depending on the spirit of the family member. If they are in full support of the fast, they are more likely to be an encouragement during the fast than if they view it as a waste of time.

I am blessed to have a wife who understands fasting. The main reason she is understanding is because she has fasted herself. She knows how hard it is to go nine days without food because she has done it. People who have fasted are more likely to understand than those who haven't. That is not meant to slight any person who isn't a fast-er because there are a lot of wonderful, understanding people who have never fasted. I also know, however, that when you have been on a God journey without food, you immediately root for someone when they start out on the same path.

The negative side to family members swaying the outcome of a fast is that they may not realize the immediate importance of the fast and thus may try to discourage you from continuing when you get weak or hungry. I think it is vital that you have the right voices speaking into your spirit when you're fasting. If you know a family member is carnal and will not understand the importance of the fast, then I recommend not bringing it up with him or her. Keep discouraging voices as far away as possible.

One of the reasons a family member's words can be crucial is if the fast-er is having a rough day, that family member, if allowed to, can either encourage the fast-er to keep going or discourage him or her to the point that the fast ends. There will be days where your willpower will not be not as strong as other days. Plan in advance on that happening. Recognize when you're weaker and try to stay positive by staying away from the negative. Don't allow them to speak doubt into your spirit.

This fast is going to work, and in the end you're going to see that your labor was not in vain! You will never be the same again, and you will never want to be the same again. Something will begin burning in you that hell fears more than anything. You have been prepared, now go after it.

## CHAPTER 5

# Beyond Motivation

Wororld-renowned ocular surgeon and author Dr. James Gills has accomplished some feats that many would acknowledge as amazing. I'm not talking about his occupation or books; I'm talking about his athletic accomplishments. Dr. Gills has proven to all aspiring athletes over the last eighty-one years that they can accomplish their dream. He has completed forty-six marathons, eighteen Boston marathons, fourteen one-hundred-mile mountain runs, and six double triathlons. He completed the last double triathlon when he was in his fifties.

A triathlon is a combination of swimming, biking, and running. In a triathlon, the competitor must first swim 2.4 miles, then bike 112 miles, and then finish the race by running a marathon, which is 26.2 miles. Obviously, a double triathlon is twice the distance of everything just mentioned. For all the non-mathematical geniuses, that is 4.8 miles of swimming, 224 miles of biking, and 52.6 miles of running. Oh, and did I mention all of this must be completed in under thirty-six hours to qualify?

When asked the secret to completing a double triathlon, Dr. Gills's answer was simple yet profound: "I talk to myself." He added that when people only listen, they can't control what they hear, but when they talk to themselves, they can control what is being said. Weeks before the race he will be talking to himself about the race, so by the time the day arrives it is already a done deal in his mind. This, in a nutshell, is what you need to do before going on a fast.

What should you say to yourself when you're about to go on a fast? A good place to start would be "I can do all things through Christ which strengtheneth me." Tell yourself daily that this is going to change your life, your family's life, and whoever else you are fasting for. Remind yourself audibly and daily that this is not going to be in vain and this fast is positioning you for greater things in God. Tell yourself that you will not quit; you will endure whatever you have to endure. Get serious about it. Like David, encourage yourself!

There is something special about talking your way out of doubt and discouragement. Hell hates that. If Satan's imps have pinned you in a corner with threats and worries, look them in the eye and say, "I'm coming out of this now!" Talk when the enemy wants you to be quiet. Goliath roared death threats and other trash to David, wanting him to shut up and stand there shaking in his boots, but the boy wasn't intimidated. He gave Goliath an earful in return. He yelled, "Today the Lord will conquer you, and I will kill you and cut off your head. And then I will give the dead bodies of your men to the birds and wild animals, and the whole world will know that there is a God in Israel!" (1 Sam. 17:46, NLT). David knew you can't be silent and hope that God comes through. When your enemy is shouting, shout back!

Some miracles come only when preceded by a verbal declaration that they will happen. The woman with the issue of blood said within herself while making her way to Jesus, "If I can just touch his robe, I will be healed" (Matt. 9:21, NLT). The original text indicates she was repeating this to herself over and over. In other words, you must talk to yourself all the way through the battle; it is essential that you keep speaking the miraculous that is going to follow the sacrifice your body is enduring.

## MOTIVATION MUST COME FROM WITHIN

Please don't attempt to go on a fast without proper motivation. Without it, you will abort the fasting mission and end up discouraged. Motivation is essential in order for you to last. I'm talking about inner motivation, not external motivation. If someone isn't walking alongside you inspiring you with every step, you're going to quit and head to Sonic for a burger. You can't count on external motivation to get the job done, but you can count on internal motivation.

Motivation gets you out of bed in the morning and prods you to get ready for work. Motivation is a fire that you must light daily in yourself to keep focused and willing to go on. Motivation keeps you positive when things around you look bleak.

This is true even as I'm writing this book. Some days I feel motivated to write; other days I would rather work on other things in my personal life. When I'm motivated to write, I can sit for hours and unleash the message that is burning inside of me. When I'm not motivated to write, I don't even want to open the laptop.

A lot of people come to church each week to get a motivational word to keep them from backsliding on Monday. They have to be motivated to keep living for the one who died on a cross for them. If the preacher doesn't hit the ball out of the park, that person may not be there Wednesday night or even the following Sunday because they left church uninspired and unmotivated. However, the problem wasn't the preacher's message; it was a lack of inner spiritual motivation on the believer's part. I like to say, "People who are always in the word, don't always need a word." The opposite must therefore be true: "If you always need a word, it's a sign that you're not spending enough time in the word." The Bible will inspire you to keep living right if you let it have more than thirty seconds of your week when the minister is reading his text.

## FASTING MOTIVATED!

"Go get it done!" I said that tonight to a friend who was entering a twenty-one day fast. "Go get it done" is what some of you need to do. You've thought about it long enough. It's time to shoot for the moon. Pray hard, dream big, and fast long! That's how you stay motivated. When entering a fast, it is essential that you fill your mind with positive input. Talk to God about it and then talk to yourself as Dr. Gills does. It makes a major difference when the motivation booming inside of you is louder than the growls of anguish issuing from your stomach. Food will be there when you're done, but right now it's time to get it done!

The motivation factor will stay with you on a fast as long as you keep feeding it. Feed it as many times as possible on a daily basis. Remind yourself that the rewards far outweigh the suffering. The change that is taking place in your life will not be temporary; it will be the launching pad to your destiny. Motivation needs to be acknowledged by you. Speak it into existence. Keep it alive!

Several friends have asked me about the secrets of fasting and what they need to do to go beyond their current limit. Each one who has heeded the advice about the motivation factor has seen incredible results, along with shattering their previously set number of days fasting. A young man who had previously fasted only one day just finished six days with water only. A pastor who had gone five days just completed a twenty-one day fast with ease. Another pastor with whom I shared the motivation factor was quite sick in his body. He was sixty-eight years old and had been fighting health issues for a long time. He completed a twenty-one-day fast with water only. Today, six years later, he is in good health and doing wonderfully well.

## MOTIVATION CAN GROW OR SHRINK

People who decide to go on an extended fast usually have a particular motivation or a specific reason for the fast. They may need an answer, a breakthrough, direction, healing, or any number of things. The initial impact of motivation, once it hits the mind of the individual, can either grow or shrink from that point on. I have experienced both the growing and the shrinking, and I can tell you that the more I talked to Jesus (or myself or my wife) about the fast the greater the motivation became. The less I prayed about it or talked to myself or my wife about it, the punier the motivation became. Listening is good if God is talking, but if he goes silent, watch out for the other voices that will speak discouragement and doubt into your spirit. Those other voices are motivation-killers; they can destroy a destiny that was about to be unlocked by simply being listened to.

## WHEN MOTIVATION BEGINS TO DIE

If the fast goes long enough, there will be a day when you wake up and no matter how you try to inspire yourself, the excitement just will not be there. This is the beginning of the death of the motivational phase. As mentioned above, motivation is fickle at times. Some days it's there; some days it's not. You have two options when you enter this phase of the fast. One, you can end the fast, as a lot of people do, or two, you can enter a new phase I call "determination."

Determination is a powerful thing to possess while on a fast. I can tell you firsthand that if you tap into determination, a ten-day fast can go twenty-one days, and a thirty-day fast can go forty. Determination is the strength to endure whatever the opposition is throwing at you. Determination wills you to keep going. The stronger your determination is, the longer you can go.

Determination is all about mental focus. What you think about, talk about, read, and listen to will decide the amount of determination that flows through you. Determination kicks in as soon as the opposition starts speaking. A word of caution: once a person begins to physically suffer during a fast, motivation begins to dwindle and sometimes the person needs to stop for health reasons. Let me be even more transparent: If you are urinating blood, stop the fast, but if you have a headache, keep going. You may find yourself entering a new spiritual dimension.

The determination phase kicks in when something says, "Stop! You won't—you can't—make it any longer!" This is the moment you find that inner drive that says, "I refuse to stop here because greater revelations, answered prayers, encounters, and breakthroughs lie ahead. I must press on; I must stay the course!" Determination will carry you when you feel like you can't take another step. Determination will look fear or pain in the eye and stare it down until it bows its head in defeat. Growing up, we used to sing the gospel song "I am determined to hold out till the end." This upbeat worship song turned Wednesday night's weary Christian soldiers into warring Christian soldiers on their way to work the next morning.

I remember on day eighteen of a twenty-one-day juice fast my kidneys felt like they were being squeezed by a giant vice grip. Everything in me was telling me to stop the fast—everything except the determination and focus on a need I had that hadn't yet been answered by the Lord. When the vice would tighten, I would drink more water or cranberry juice. There was no way I was stopping until God met the need. God gave me supernatural strength those last three days, then he answered my prayer in an undeniable fashion.

Our determination has to be stronger than the opposition's determination. I know everyone doesn't agree with the following statement, but I would rather die than eat when I'm close to something in the Spirit after a few days of fasting. If I think I have God's attention and I can sense an imminent breakthrough, someone would have to drag me from the arena, because, for me, the fight is to the death. We need soldiers who, after the battle is ended, will still be standing over their headless enemy lying in the dirt.

## STAYING DETERMINED

I am often asked the question, "How does one stay determined once the fast has entered that grueling, miserable stage?" The answer is quite simple: stay focused on what you are fasting for. The duration of your determination is commensurate with how focused you remain on the needs of others and yourself as you fast, as well as the reminder that with each meal rejected you are one step closer to the answer. I tell myself things like "This person still needs to be healed" or "This situation still hasn't changed" or "I haven't yet received direction from the Lord on this decision." These things keep me focused and determined not to eat. I also keep in mind that if I eat, the food will satisfy my appetite for only an hour or two before my stomach begins grumbling for more. Why give up something so eternally impacting for a bowl of soup when God hasn't released you from your fast? If Esau were alive today, I believe he would advise you to keep pursuing your answer because the food isn't nearly as good as that miracle you're needing!

Nothing will bolster your determination like the revelation that you are closer to the Lord than you've ever been and that if you continue the fast, you will draw even closer. When you open your Bible during a fast, the words jump off the pages and arrest your thinking to let you know the word is alive, it is aimed at you, and your life is under the all-seeing eye of the Lord. You will receive revelations from the Lord—and about the Lord—that you wouldn't see at any other time.

Another channel through which determination will flow into your spirit is the realization that the spirit world is paying close attention to you. The encounters I've had while fasting are mind blowing. I will share some later in this book, but for now, I will say that your sensitivity to the "other world" heightens to a new level. To be even more transparent, when I go on a long fast, I expect some type of encounter during or after the fast either with the Lord, his angels, or a spirit from hell. It doesn't happen every time, but I always expect something to manifest. When Jesus ended his forty-day fast, he faced Satan head on and then was ministered to by angels.

## ENTER SELF-DISCIPLINE

In this chapter we have discussed motivation and determination. Now let's turn our attention to a third essential element for lasting on any fast. You must settle in your spirit that you want to remain in this territory after the fast is completed. This sacred territory is called self-discipline. It is a place that must be visited during the fast and dwelt in afterward.

Self-discipline will add strength after motivation begins to wither and determination ebbs. There will be a day (or two or three) when you have to get up, as miserable as you feel, and remind yourself, "I made this decision when I was in my right mind. I will endure to the end of this fast by keeping to my spiritual routine and by exercising self-discipline." Self-discipline prioritizes your life.

David Campbell once said, "Discipline is remembering what you want." I couldn't agree more. Whether it is eating salad when you're craving junk food; putting the extra ten dollars toward paying a bill instead of splurging on a coffee run; waking up to pray when you would rather roll over and keep dreaming; working on a book (personal note to myself) instead of relaxing after the kids are asleep; or fasting when you want to pig out, self-discipline will keep you focused on the end goal. When you view your giant opponents through the lens of self-discipline, they will look like grasshoppers.

As I was pondering the value of self-discipline, my thoughts drifted until I thought about my father in Alaska. To me he is the epitome of self-discipline. He reads the entire Bible through every thirty days and has done so for over thirty years. Seven days a week, 365 days a year you'll find him reading that Bible. I know of no other human being on the planet who reads their Bible through twelve times a year, every year. On top of that, for several years now, he doesn't eat for twelve hours each day, seven days a week, 365 days a year. This does not include his extended fasts of thirty and forty days.

I asked him recently about the discipline factor in his life and how he keeps it up year after year. He told me that years ago he vowed to the Lord that he would read the Bible through every thirty days and not eat for twelve hours each day, and he stays focused on that vow every day. I'm not suggesting this to anyone reading this book; this is his personal calling and commitment to God. I will say, however, that we all need something to dwell on daily to keep us focused on our destiny.

Disciplined commitment is the distance between dreams and destiny. If we attempt some great feat with desire only and leave discipline out of the equation, we probably will fail. Zig Ziglar once said, "It was character that got us out of bed, commitment that moved us into action, and discipline that enabled us to follow through." Discipline is the "closer factor." Every baseball team has a closer—a pitcher who specializes in getting the final outs in a close game when his team is in the lead.

You've probably heard the quote, "Discipline is doing what needs to be done, even though you don't want to." How true! As mentioned earlier, on the days of a fast when you'd rather be doing anything but fasting, the discipline of staying focused will not go unrewarded. In fact, the reward will be so great that if you keep going, you'll look back at your moment of mental weakness and thank the Lord for keeping you on the path to his perfect will in your life.

Several friends of mine are big into fasting and they all have one thing in common: they practice self-discipline in their daily lives. Whether or not they are fasting, I know they're doing certain things every day: they are praying, they are reading their Bibles, and they are pursuing God with a hunger that can be described only as undeniable desire. Even though they all have accomplished incredible things for the kingdom, you would never be able to tell it because they're not satisfied with where they have been. They are consistently craving more of the presence of the Lord.

Someone once said that the definition of insanity is doing the same thing over and over while expecting a different outcome. I would like to add the definition of spiritual insanity: it is to do nothing every day to pursue God and his glory, yet expect to have more of God and his glory. I have learned that if I maintain self-discipline on the fast, I can expect results. God has always honored principles more than personality, persuasion, or popularity. Godly principles will work, and disciplining your body to fast for a greater relationship with the Lord is most definitely a godly principle. Dreams will come true if you discipline your life for their outcome.

> *The vehicle that drives your dreams*
> *from desire into destiny is called discipline.*

The above quote was given to me by the Lord late one night while writing this book. Discipline is like a transportation system; it takes you and all of your dreams on a journey through every terrain and obstacle in the way, and then drops you off at the place called fulfillment. When you embark on your next fast, let discipline be the pilot of your mind. You will not crash and you will make it to your destination safely.

## THE GOD STRENGTH FACTOR

When it comes to the length of your fast, this is the decisive factor. It trumps motivation, determination, and even self-discipline. I call it the God Strength Factor. If God gives you the strength to fast ten days, then you will be able to do it. You may stop short of the ten days if your motivation, determination, and self-discipline fade, but the strength will be there.

That being said, once God has decided you have fasted long enough, his strength to continue fasting will lift, making it difficult for you to keep going. You may have planned to go fourteen days, but God may tell you on day nine that it's time to get off the altar because your prayer has been heard. How will you be able to tell? You will be released from the fast mentally. In other words, you will no longer desire to fast.

The moment the desire to fast lifts from you, your mind immediately feels to end the fast, and continuing now seems frustrating. This is proof that the supernatural strength and wisdom of our God is watching and helping us in our daily lives. I have been on several fasts where I was trying to go a certain number of days but then I would feel the strength lift and I knew it was over. I knew I could no longer continue, no matter how disciplined I was because I would now be trying to finish the fast on human will power alone.

## EXPOSING PRIDE

This leads me to a very important quality that can be destroyed or enhanced by fasting—pride. Pride can come into play if God has released you from a fast, but instead of breaking the fast, you continue fasting because you want to be able to say you fasted a certain number of days. The problem with "over fasting" (going beyond what God is telling you to do) can become dangerous both spiritually and physically.

Whatever you gained in the days spent fasting with the help of God's strength can be lost by going "past God," as in "go two steps forward, then three steps backward." Your fast was meant to yield a reward from your heavenly Father, but after receiving your discharge papers, you stayed in the war instead of taking the rest and relaxation he wanted you to have. Careful, soldier. If God says you're done, trust him. He is protecting you.

Basically, the humility-based fast of pursuing God and his direction can become a prideful agenda of competition and self-exaltation. The enemy knows the power of fasting so it makes sense when he tries to con you into going too far. If he knows you are so driven that you won't give up, he's going to try to lure you beyond your limits and kill you through exhaustion.

Physical problems can result when you try to continue a fast God has told you to stop. Fasting, if not done properly, can wreak havoc with your internal organs. I don't mean you'll get sick every time you fast longer than what God intended for that particular fast, but it has happened more than once to people I have known. Maybe God was releasing you from the fast to keep your kidneys from failing or your intestines from becoming impaired. The writer said, "In everything give thanks"; that is, even when God says stop and everything in you wants to keep going. Thank him for loving you enough to protect you.

Just because God stops you from going forty days this time does not mean you aren't destined to go on a forty-day fast in your future. The first time I attempted to fast fourteen days, I only made it eight. God released me and I knew it. The next time I made it nine days; the following time, ten days. Each time I attempted a prolonged fast, I made it one more day: eleven, twelve, thirteen. Yet I kept banging on the door. I was determined to get to fourteen somehow. The next fast I went forty days, not fourteen. God's strength allowed me to go from thirteen days to forty days. The same God who strengthened me to fast forty days in 2013 is the same God that gave me strength to fast thirteen days earlier that same year.

Sometimes I wonder if God couldn't trust me with forty days or even fourteen days, and then, after several futile attempts, he granted me strength to endure longer than I ever dreamed possible. Sometimes I have to pray that God will be able to trust me with more, either because I feel I'm not ready, or, for some reason, I'm being held back from something I desire.

God will trust us once we prove to him that we won't take advantage of his favor. Some people beg God for answers and then, once they tap into his favor, they lose all desperation to know him in a greater measure. The truth is their search was never for him but rather for his blessings. If I'm going to walk in the authority and favor that come through extended fasting, I'm going to have to walk humbly. If my head is going to swell due to accomplishing something he gave me the strength to fulfill, I would rather have him tap me on the shoulder and release me from something destructive that could be waiting to prey upon my spirit.

I'm not trying to discourage the reader from attempting a lengthy fast; I'm merely stating that should you feel released from a fast and you know the release came from the Lord, go ahead and eat. There's nothing wrong with living to fight another day. There will be other battles and other fasts that will last longer. Take the territory he is granting you and be thankful that he strengthened you as long as he did.

In summary, entering a fast requires motivation. You must talk to yourself and stay positive as long as possible, because, if motivation dies and determination doesn't kick in, you are done. Determination will help you to stay on the fast, along with self-discipline to endure the last few days and hours of the fast. Above all, God's strength will carry you beyond motivation, beyond determination, and beyond self-discipline, for his strength is made perfect in your weakness. The next time you are planning a fast, pray for his strength to come upon you. If you will do everything you can and then depend on his strength, you're going to accomplish something great for his kingdom.

## CHAPTER 6
## Climbing Everest

It was around 10:30 p.m. on Sunday night, July 14, 2013, when I received the phone call that would forever change my walk with the Lord. My wife, Jenee, and I were driving home from a revival service we had just preached in Jacksonville, Florida. At the time, we lived in Ocala, Florida, a two-hour drive from Jacksonville. For once, we wanted to go home and sleep in our own bed after church.

When my cell phone rang, I looked at the caller ID, and it was a pastor friend named John Martin from Muncie, Indiana. I had preached several revivals in his church, and that was where I met my lovely bride, for she and her family attended there. I answered the phone, and we small-talked for a few seconds before he told me the reason for his call; he wanted to share with me the message he had preached that morning. He said, "Josh, this is right up your alley." I listened as he described his message about climbing Mount Everest.

Mount Everest, at 29,035 feet above sea level, is the tallest elevation on earth. John Martin described the dangers that climbers encounter on the great mountain. It is not a vacation spot!

Exposure to storms, wind, ice, snow, avalanches, oxygen deprivation, falls, frostbite, or sub-zero temperatures have taken the lives of over three hundred individuals, including Sherpas from Nepal and climbers from around the world.

Most of the calendar year it's impossible to scale the mountains due to extreme weather conditions. There are only a couple of small windows each year when the weather calms down enough to give climbers a chance to reach the summit. The first window usually arrives around the last week of April or the first part of May, and the second window usually comes in October. John Martin used these windows of opportunity as an analogy for going higher in the Spirit. During the times when the windows are open, we can reach places and see things in God we've never experienced before.

Once he commented about windows of opportunity to go higher in God, his voice seemed to fade and I heard the voice of the Lord say, "You will fast forty days either now or never. You will begin in two weeks at midnight on July 29, and you will finish September 6 at midnight." Then the Lord's voice faded and I heard my friend still speaking on the other end of the line.

I was stunned, shocked, scared, and stoked all at the same time. Could this really be God? I had never gone without food for even fourteen days. How could God expect me to climb my spiritual Everest when I hadn't even finished those shorter fasts in my past? If I was going to complete forty days, it would have to be a calling, and God would have to give me strength to do it. I had always dreamed of fasting forty days someday; but not at thirty years old. Not here, not now.

I had two weeks to prepare for the longest fast I had ever attempted, and I had no idea what was in store. I began to study every verse in the Bible on fasting. I read every book I could get my hands on that dealt with fasting and then wrote down everything I could remember about fasting. I knew if I was going to climb this spiritual Everest, I needed to be psyched.

Moses climbed Mount Sinai twice while fasting, so why wouldn't I be able to? I studied everything in the Bible that took forty days to accomplish. I wrote down every verse I could find that involved forty days. Rereading those verses every day became an encouragement during my fast.

> *And it came to pass at the end of forty days, that Noah opened the window of the ark which he had made.* (Gen. 8:6)

The above verse became the first verse I read every day. Some things can be seen only after the forty-day mark; when the forty-first day arrives, the window is ready to be opened. God had shut the door of the ark and they were in it for the ride. But after the flood waters had abated and the ark landed on Mount Ararat, they waited forty days for the moment to begin to see out. Sometimes you have to wait things out, but once you endure the wait, the time comes for fresh vision. You can clearly see that you're going to get out of that ark.

There are several other examples about the importance of forty days, such as in Exodus 24, where Moses was in the midst of the cloud with God for forty days, and Deuteronomy 9, where Moses was given the two tables of stone containing the Ten Commandments after forty days and nights of fasting. I could go into detail of how Acts 1 tells us that Jesus stayed for forty days after he resurrected from the grave. I could describe Elijah's forty-day fast that began with an encounter with an angel and ended with an encounter with God.

There are many examples to choose from, but I want to visit the story of how David endured a forty-day waiting game prior to his famous bout with the Philistine champion.

*And the Philistine drew near morning and evening, and presented himself forty days.* (1 Sam. 17:16)

Goliath, the enemy of God's people, came out two times a day for forty days to intimidate and terrify the Israelites and berate their God. (Maybe the enemy has been haranguing you and trashing your God. I wonder what or who might show up on day forty-one to fight for you!) No one in Saul's army dared to accept the challenge until the fortieth day. Goliath should have packed up his armor and weapons on day thirty-nine and gone home, because when God is through, you are through.

After forty days the answer came in the form of a teenager who showed up at the Israelite camp bearing parched corn and bread for his soldier brothers, and cheeses for their captain. Eliab, David's oldest brother, berated David: "What are doing around here anyway? . . . I know about your pride and deceit. You just want to see the battle" (1 Sam. 17:28, NLT). David showed his brothers, King Saul, and the entire Israelite army what real courage and trust in God could do. He went out and killed the giant. It was the biggest foe he had ever encountered.

Mount Everest was the only thing I could compare this fast to because it was the biggest thing I had ever encountered in the Spirit. It was the Goliath that I had to conquer. I studied Everest and what it took to climb to the summit. I wanted to know every detail possible before I began.

## THE DEATH ZONE

The first thing that stood out to me about climbing Everest is that near the summit there is a two-thousand-foot razor-edged hill composed of ice. Most climbers refer to this hill as the death zone because many of the people who have perished on Everest have died there. The oxygen level at that altitude is not sufficient to sustain human life. If a climber stays there too long, tragedy can result due to loss of vital functions or poor decisions made under stress and weakness.

How long is too long? The average person can endure only twenty minutes on the summit of Everest and then has to come down. In other words, the environment at that altitude is so hostile that your body cannot acclimatize. It uses oxygen faster than it can be replenished. Climbers stay at the summit only long enough to take a few pictures, maybe leave a memento, and experience the view from the top of the world.

When you go on a forty-day fast, please understand that once you've achieved it, enjoy your triumph for a moment and then come down. No one in the Bible fasted longer than forty days, not even Jesus. Moses fasted forty days twice but had a break in between each fast at the forty-day mark.

The human body begins to hunger after forty days without food. You are probably thinking your body hungers after forty minutes, but what most of us describe as hunger is actually thirst. Your body is used to being fed at certain times, so you assume when you miss a meal that you're starving when you really aren't. But after forty days your body begins to hunger; it needs food to sustain life. Going longer than that becomes dangerous—death-zone dangerous.

## LIVING ON THE MOUNTAIN

At the base of Everest are villages, many inhabitants of which are people known as Sherpas. Sherpas are the most elite mountain climbers in the world. They are usually in incredible physical condition and can outclimb anyone coming to conquer the great mountain they live on. They can climb with greater speed because they're used to the altitude of the mountains. They live in the environment that others only visit for a temporary climb.

These warriors are incredibly useful for climbers attempting to scale Everest, because they plan the route, rig hold ropes, and carry the climbing kit (i.e., food, gas for cooking, tents, sleeping bags, water purifier). When climbers reach a new base point during the climb, the Sherpa has been there beforehand setting everything up, and has moved on to a higher elevation to once again prepare the way. These efforts of bravery can cost the Sherpas their lives as they tackle the elements alone.

I am intrigued by these Sherpas because I can quickly see the spiritual correlation to their value. Some people are like the climbers who come once year or once in a lifetime. These types of people consecrate themselves once in a while and will attempt a sacrificial journey, but they don't live sacrificially. In contrast, the Sherpas are a representation of the type of people who live on the mountain.

Let me add that if you're going to walk in the Spirit, you must learn to first step into the Spirit every time you are near his presence. Have you ever wondered why you can get up in the morning and pray and feel like a changed individual while you are praying, only to feel like the same old carnal you three hours later? I've learned that when this happens to me, I simply haven't been in his presence long enough during my morning prayer session.

Perhaps I was tired or frustrated with something and therefore forfeited my chance to walk in the Spirit the rest of the day. I thought, "Hey, I prayed an hour. I didn't get a breakthrough, but at least I prayed."

It is commendable to pray when we don't feel like it, but all too often we aren't feeling like it when we go into prayer and therefore we stay with our feet planted on terra firma, and our prayers barely make it to the ceiling.

Prayer without sincerely desiring an encounter with the Lord will leave you walking in the flesh after you're done. I'm tired of breakthroughs that last only a few hours. I want to live on the mountain and walk in the Spirit. It's time to start pursuing Jesus like never before! It is time to walk in the Spirit. Don't waste another prayer meeting or another service or another altar call by simply leaving his presence while still in the flesh.

People who are consecrating consistently are like spiritual Sherpas who live on the mountain. I want to be like that. I want to be able to help others on their spiritual journeys. I'm not interested in just climbing and seeing the view from the mountaintop and then never telling anyone or encouraging anyone in their attempts to reach the top. In fact, that's the reason I'm writing this book; I want this book to serve as oxygen for your climb. I want it to be the rope you hold onto in the toughest part of the climb. You can do this! I believe in you and, more important, Jesus believes in you. In fact, he wants you to do this more often than you do. He is for you!

## YOU NEED A COACH

Find someone who has been where you want to go. You will find that when you have someone rooting for you who understands the battle you are fighting, your focus will last longer. It is a blessing to have someone who can advise you and strengthen you in the tough moments of the climb.

Someone has climbed ahead of you and prepared the route. Someone has words that will intensify your hunger for the things of the Spirit. Pray that the Lord will send you the person who will be able to inspire you and strengthen you. If you are planning a longer fast in the near future, you need someone to be accountable to.

Never let hell convince you to take on a spiritual Everest uncovered. You need someone who wants you to go all the way but can stop you if they notice you struggling with your health. Hikers at base camp on Everest check in multiple times a day with their guides, the Sherpas, who are up ahead gaging the winds, checking the route, and noting things the climber will encounter. Your pastor should come to mind as you read this. You need to keep the line of communication open with your pastor. He is watching the landscape of the Everest you're trying to climb. As you climb, you need protection from enemies and predators that inhabit Everest.

## CLIMBERS IN THE KINGDOM

Your age doesn't matter when it comes to consecrating for the Lord. Anyone can make the journey. Anyone can climb the mountain. Jordan Romero became the youngest person to summit Everest at the age of thirteen. He had already climbed Kilimanjaro at the age of ten. This young man obviously grew up on mountains to be able to accomplish such feats at such a tender age.

When it comes to climbing in the Spirit, you don't have to wait until you reach forty to reach for the things of God. I know young people who have gone on extended fasts while in high school. It's all about how badly you want it. There is a cry from the Spirit searching for the next climber in the kingdom. Will it be you? Are you going to press while others relax? God's voice is calling and someone is going to hear it. They are going to put on their climbing boots, collect their gear, and declare war on hell.

To me, fasting is a closer spiritual equivalent to climbing than any other physical activity. I say this because fasting changes your position more quickly than any other spiritual endeavor. Fasting elevates you in the spirit world, enabling you to see things from a higher point of view—God's point of view. I believe that people have never been closer to God than when they've been on a long journey of prayer and fasting. Just as the ability to continue the climb as exhaustion overtakes you, so too is the ability to stay focused on a fast when your body is weakening by the minute.

Another similarity to climbing is the fact that you must set your own pace. You might have a health issue that requires you to have a certain type of nutritional element in your body each day. You might not be able to do water only or juice only. That doesn't mean you have an excuse not to do what you can do for his kingdom. Don't stay at base camp and compare yourself to climbers who have accomplished incredible feats for God while you've never missed a snack in thirty-six years. Get up and go after it. Where can you climb? What can you do to go higher? Do it now!

## CHAPTER 7

## Find Your Runway

As a full-time evangelist traveling across the globe, I can often be sighted in airports waiting for my next flight—usually to somewhere cold in the winter or hot in the summer. I'm not complaining, though. I'm sure Paul gladly would have traded schedules and means of transportation with me. Considering the times when the ship he was aboard ran aground or sank, I'm almost positive he gladly would have waited in line to sit in coach for several hours to go preach somewhere that didn't involve being beaten and arrested at the end of the flight.

We have it easy in today's modern society. Huge planes fly us or modern vehicles drive us to wherever we want to go. We stay in hotels with king-size beds. Somehow I don't see the apostles complaining to the Samaritan innkeeper about not having enough towels when they were holding a revival there; but who knows, maybe they did.

Most weekends I'm flying on airplanes, often in a seat like 36B near the restrooms at the tail of the plane. I have a pre-flight ritual. First, when boarding, I touch the outside of the plane as

I step inside and say a prayer over the flight. Second, as we head toward the runway, I repent of any sin that could be in my life. Third, I speak to the spirit world as the wheels lift off that no evil spirit is allowed to follow me to my destination. Fourth, when the plane lands I speak to the spirit-world inhabitants of any state or nation I've just entered and take authority over that region in Jesus' name. When you travel for Jesus as often as I do, you're bound to have some encounters with hell, and I've had more than my share, to put it mildly. I'll relate some of these experiences later in the book.

To me, the most exciting part of the flight is the takeoff as the plane lumbers down the runway, gathering momentum as it prepares to soar. This brings me to the subject of this chapter—the importance of the runway. The runway must be long for multiple reasons. First and foremost, a plane can take off only if the force of lift is stronger than the force of the plane's weight. The longer the runway, the more momentum and speed are gathered by the aircraft before attempting to rise from the surface of the earth.

A runway can be compared to extended fasting because it serves as a runway in the spirit world. In order to gain momentum with God before your ministry does with man, you must find your runway—the longest runway you can find. In other words, go on the longest fast possible. Nothing will cause you to soar in the Spirit like a runway paved out of fasting.

The spirit world is more real than the world you live in. Angels and demons inhabit this place, and if you're going to soar into their world to do something for the kingdom of heaven, you're going to have to learn to pray and fast. Things and beings that are invisible and seemingly nonexistent to the carnal person become alarmingly real to the man or woman who is gaining speed on the runway. This book is not designed to frighten anyone, but the simple fact is that the more you fast and pray, the more of the spirit world you will hear and see.

## TAXIING BEFORE TAKEOFF

The plane is pushed away from the gate and slowly turns to head toward the runway. This has spiritual implications as well. Usually when a long fast is on the horizon for me, I begin to feel gradual movement toward it in my spirit. I know the fast isn't going to begin that day, but I definitely can feel the plane starting to move.

The plane begins to roll toward the runway, and you think it's finally time for takeoff. Suddenly, after taxiing for a few minutes, the plane slows to a halt. Then you hear the pilot's voice over the intercom informing the passengers, "We are third, fourth, or [fill in the blank] in line for takeoff." You were expecting a roaring takeoff down the runway before soaring into the sky, but there are other planes in the way at the current moment. It's not that you aren't about to soar; it's that you're being delayed for a few more minutes. What does this have to do with fasting? There will be times when you're so ready to fast. You're excited and motivated beyond words! Then something comes up and you have to put it off for a bit. Nothing frustrates you more. You want to take off now, but God says to wait. Why? He's protecting you from something you can't see with your human spirit, or, in our terms, in seat 36B.

This is where I've failed multiple times, because when the plane stops, I still want to take off. In the fasting world, this means I attempt to go on the fast without gathering momentum on the runway. It's hard to get anywhere when the plane isn't moving.

## YOU WILL TAKEOFF

I can assure you that you're going to do this fast. When it comes to God and his plans for your life, being delayed has never meant being denied. I'm talking to the warriors, the ones whose thoughts are focused on this fast. Casual consecrators probably won't connect with me at this moment, but to the hungry, let it be declared into the spirit world that you're going to do this. I speak it into your life right at this moment. There is about to be a shift in your spirit and in your mind that propels you to the runway.

God knows how hungry you are to do this because he placed the hunger there. He wants you to want him. He wants you to search for the secret place. When you reach the place where this is all you can think about, the plane is starting to taxi, so get ready! I know from personal experience that when God holds you up for a few days, weeks, or even months, he will eventually release you to start down the runway with his fuel in your spiritual gas tank. It isn't a matter of if; it's a matter of when.

## SOARING IN THE SPIRIT

It's amazing how quickly an airplane can reach a cruising altitude of thirty thousand feet just a few minutes after takeoff. The runway didn't just provide momentum for a nice takeoff; it has catapulted the plane far above the clouds. From this height the runway now seems small and insignificant, but if it hadn't been for that runway, the plane would still be sitting on the tarmac. The point is that fasting catapults you to places in the spirit world. You will be amazed at how quickly God's favor, which has always hovered above you (like the clouds) but has never been on you, is now all around you.

In hindsight, after the fast is completed it seems like it was just a small sacrifice to make; however, small sacrifices now can engender major favor later. David didn't think that taking his brothers some food before the battle would have any bearing on his future, but what he didn't know was that the trip would involve giant-killing. He didn't realize that his destiny was connected to this lowly act of service. He obeyed his father and took food for others to eat, then slew the giant and later became king. Others ate, but David sacrificed. Think about it. What reward do you want? I can tell you that the rewards of fasting far outweigh the benefits of feasting.

## WHAT IS YOUR CRUISING ALTITUDE?

I'm on board a soaring jet headed toward my next revival. When the plane reaches a certain height above sea level, I hear the pilot's voice over the intercom: "Ladies and gentlemen, this is your captain speaking. We have reached a cruising altitude of thirty-two thousand feet. When you see the seat belt sign go off, feel free to move about the cabin when necessary." Cruising altitudes can vary, but the higher the altitude the less drag on the plane, which requires less fuel. On the other hand, the higher the altitude the longer the climb, which requires more fuel. When pilots reach an optimum cruising altitude, they've arrived at the "sweet spot"—flying as high as possible as fast as possible while burning the least amount of fuel. This is the level (or in spiritual terms, the dimension) where most of the flight takes place.

The pilot doesn't attempt to cruise at a level where there is a lot of air traffic. Once the pilot hast taken the plane to a cruising altitude, the air traffic controller informs the pilot that it's now safe to cruise. This doesn't mean the pilot can go to sleep but rather that he has taken the plane into a dimension that has less air traffic and can now cruise safely.

Once you have done enough fasting (climbing), you enter a dimension that has less human air traffic. This doesn't mean you can go to sleep spiritually and just coast into your destiny; it means you have reached cruising altitude and can now flow with what happens in the Spirit.

There are times during the flight when the pilot must climb another thousand feet due to another plane in the area or if there is air turbulence ahead. This is referred to as step climbing. The pilot doesn't need to climb several thousand feet and establish a new cruising altitude; he just needs to avoid potential problems in the pathway of the plane he is flying.

When you get to cruising altitude in your ministry or calling, there will be times when you have to adjust to something coming in the atmosphere. This is easier to do when you've already climbed to a place where you know what you're doing in this dimension. Things will invade your cruising altitude from time to time: sometimes it's something identifiable; other times it's not.

For instance, turbulence is invisible, but another aircraft coming at you is visible. In the spiritual dimension you will have to adjust your cruising altitude when encountering things you can see or things you can't see but you can feel. You feel the effects of turbulence but can't necessarily see the wind causing it. My point is that when you arrive at the place where you're cruising for God, you'll have to make adjustments from time to time to avoid catastrophe.

Some things will be clearly visible, and when you see them approaching you know you need to go just a little higher. Others things will be impossible to see, but you can sense them coming at you. If you don't adjust your altitude to avoid the turbulence, your cruising level will feel more like a roller coaster invented by a maniac demon. The flight of life is never going to be easy, not even after a long fast that propels you upward to your cruising altitude. You must make adjustments "on the fly" (pun intended) or you won't finish the flight where you want to land.

However, if you remain focused while you're cruising and doing great exploits for the Lord, you can see more clearly the things that are approaching because you're no longer climbing to get somewhere; you've already reached cruising altitude. Also, you can now feel things coming that are invisible to others, people who, in fact, don't comprehend the existence of this level of activity because it exists and moves in the air above where they dwell.

This dimension comes only through prayer and fasting. Remember that we wrestle things in "high places." You can't wrestle with things in high places if you refuse to find your runway. If you're wrestling with your flesh, you need to find a runway to the spirit world so you can fulfill the destiny God has prepared for you. You want to see angels? You want to cast out devils? It has to come through prayer and fasting. You want to cruise in the Spirit? You must lift off the runway and climb to get there. Come on, God is waiting. I hear the air traffic controller calling your name. You're next in line for takeoff. God is calling you to a fast.

## HEAVEN IS PROMOTING THIS FAST

Elijah's runway and the forty-day fast he went on are quite fascinating to me because of how they began. It started with a meal cooked by an angel and an announcement sent from heaven; the angel not only cooked for him but delivered a message along with dinner. The message? "After you eat tonight, you are going on a forty-day journey." I truly believe there is a fast that is initiated by a heavenly order. Like Elijah, you are ready for it.

> *And the angel of the Lord came again the second time,*
> *and touched him, and said, Arise and eat; because the jour-*
> *ney is too great for thee.* (1 Kings 19:7)

Why was it necessary for a heavenly messenger to announce this fast? Why didn't Elijah just naturally think it was time for him to consecrate? I believe the explanation was that there would be no food available from the time he left the shade of the juniper tree he was resting under to the cave where he would have his next encounter with God. The angel knew this; Elijah did not. If Elijah had left the juniper tree without the angel's dinner announcement, he would have gotten hungry and would have searched for food that didn't exist. He now would add starvation to the frustration and depression he was already struggling with.

Anytime you feel frustrated about something spiritually and then can't seem to feel God's touch or hear God's voice afterward, you will begin to pursue spiritual food that doesn't exist. Make no mistake about it: there will be seasons when God is silent, and if you haven't eaten under your juniper tree in preparation for the journey, you'll become spiritually suicidal and think that what is actually a temporary test is none other than a permanent reality for your future.

## THE WHISPERING GOD

Elijah staggered into a cave in the crags of rugged Mount Sinai and spent the night. The next morning the first thing he heard was the voice of God: "What are you doing here, Elijah?" The discouraged, exhausted prophet replied, "I've served you zealously, but your people have torn down your altars and killed every one of your prophets, and I'm the only one left!" God replied, "Go stand at the opening of the cave."

Elijah stepped out into the dawn, only to be nearly bowled over by windstorm. It was so violent that it dislodged rocks, which plummeted down the mountainside. Then the ground began to tremble and heave, and Elijah realized he was experiencing an earthquake. No sooner had the earth quieted than a fireball roared by. Through all the upheaval, there was no voice of God. Elijah stood among the wreckage in the sudden quietness until he heard a gentle whisper and recognized it as the voice of the Lord. "What are you doing here, Elijah?" The prophet uttered the same sad litany of how he was the only prophet left. Instead of sympathy, God told him in no uncertain terms to resume his ministry; he was to go to the wilderness of Damascus and anoint the next king of Aram; he was to anoint Jehu to be the next king of Israel; he was to anoint a successor, Elishah, son of Shaphat. Then came the clincher: "I will preserve 7,000 others in Israel who have never bowed down to Baal." (See 1 Kings 19, NLT.)

This brings me to an important point. God's Spirit caused the wind to blow vehemently, the earth to quake violently, and the fire to burn volcanically. Yet God was not in these natural phenomena. Had Elijah not been connected to the Spirit through fasting, he could have mistaken these manifestations caused by the Spirit to be the voice of the Spirit. Fasting creates a sensitivity to the voice of God that can come no other way. Some of the situations and people moving around in your life at the moment may have God's Spirit near them but they may not actually carry the will of God for your life in them.

Fasting causes you to know the difference between the wind and the whispers. One is moving around you, but the other is speaking inside of you. How many times have you missed encounters with the whispering God because you ran with the wind? The wind blows, the earth quakes, the fire burns, but God whispers.

He whispers through the word, in prayer, through preaching, in dreams, in nature, through people, in meditating on him, through angels, through a book, and so many other ways. If you will listen, he will reveal things to you. Many people just want him to listen to their requests and then the prayer meeting is over. If you will put him first, you can count on him to deal with the things you're facing. After all, he is your Father.

## OUR FATHER

The disciples came to Jesus and asked him to teach them to pray. The first two words the Lord instructed the disciples to pray were "Our Father." This harks back to the previous paragraph of what God is and who he is to us. Notice the Lord did not tell them to say, "Our Savior" or "Our God" or "Our Lord" or even "Our Creator," although he is all of those things and more. He said, "I want you to think of me as your Father."

In other words, acknowledging his lordship, saving power, and creative abilities doesn't do as much for God as us telling him, "Lord, you are my Father." Why? Because every good father knows that one of the greatest, most important attributes of being a good father is having an open relationship with his child where they can communicate with him anytime about anything.

God is our Lord and Savior, but he wants us to know we are more to him than a servant in his kingdom. We have entered sonship with the King of kings and the Lord of lords. We need to fear his power and honor his lordship, but we need to come to him as our Father.

Notice also that he told them to pray "Our Father," not "My Father." He wants us to know we are all his kids. The next time you go to him to complain about someone else who is also serving him, maybe you should just say, "Our Father," and then think about the implications of that before you say another word.

## NECESSARY LAYOVERS

Every time I book airfare tickets for my scheduled revivals, crusades, or conferences, I always check for nonstop flights. If the nonstop flight doesn't cost much more than a flight involving layovers, I purchase the ticket for the nonstop flight. I've traveled enough with my family to know that the sooner we land at our destination the sooner we can rest and get focused on what God has sent us to do. This makes travel so much more enjoyable for me personally. I love knowing that when I finally escape the confines of seat 36B that I won't be getting on another plane that day.

The shorter the flight time the better I like it, but obviously, this isn't always possible because of the airline's preselected flight patterns. If nonstop flights to the destination I need are not available, I will have a necessary layover. Layovers can be refreshing if they're short and if the next flight is in close proximity to the gate where I just exited the plane. On the other hand, layovers can be stressful if these variables are missing from the equation.

In the spirit world, layovers are necessary. There will be times when you're eager to be soaring toward your destiny, but God will ground you on a layover. It may seem unnecessary to you, but his thoughts are above yours. He knows things about your future flight patterns that you don't.

## CHAPTER 8

## Fasting in Secret

This chapter was birthed late one Saturday night in 2018 in a room at Homewood Suites. My wife and children were sleeping, while I lay on the floor between the bed and the bathroom. I was reading the following scripture passage, which I've read more times than I can count.

*Moreover when ye fast, be not, as the hypocrites, of a sad countenance: for they disfigure their faces, that they may appear unto men to fast. Verily I say unto you, They have their reward. But thou, when thou fastest, anoint thine head, and wash thy face; that thou appear not unto men to fast, but unto thy father which is in secret: and thy Father, which seeth in secret, shall reward thee openly.* (Matt. 6:16–18)

As I read these verses, the Lord began to convict me as he revealed to me the importance of fasting in secret. I would like to share with you what he shared with me that evening.

Fasting was no longer a problem for me. I had gone on so many fasts that I felt I had accomplished the will of God in that area of consecration for my life. However, keeping my fasts a secret—that was something new. I always seemed to "let it be known" when I was on a fast.

I obviously had preached on the power of fasting and had alluded to several personal stories (some of which are included in this book) that had happened either during a fast or because of the fasts God has led me to complete. That apparently wasn't what was upsetting the Lord that night. He was letting me know that he wasn't pleased with my tendency to tell people when I was fasting, especially if the fast was an extended one. God's revelation in his word that night has since changed my life completely. Therefore, I feel it is important that I share with you the following essentials you need when you go on an extended fast.

## GET A FACE LIFT

The first thing Jesus focused on as essential for someone going on a fast is the importance of smiling. He instructed, "While you're fasting, do not appear to be sad." In other words, "If you're fasting, cheer up! Be happy! Be thankful you have been privileged to be chosen to accomplish this in the Spirit!" Going around with a sad countenance, Jesus said, is hypocritical behavior. Hypocrites seem to enjoy the attention they derive from others. Instead of receiving a reward from God for their efforts, their reward comes from the people around them.

Jesus said that hypocrites disfigure their faces while they're fasting. In the original Greek, the word "disfigure" is aphanizo, meaning "to snatch out of sight, to put out of view, to make unseen." This tells us they literally covered their faces in public as a signal that they were fasting. They wanted everyone who saw them to think they were consecrating themselves to the Lord. Instead, the opposite was true: they had lost focus on the Lord and were focusing on the attention of people. It is possible to lose focus while fasting, which changes the goal of pursuing God to pursuing the affirmation of man.

## GET A FACIAL

Jesus said that people who are fasting should anoint their heads and wash their faces. In other words, don't draw attention to yourself, and don't desire praise from the public. You don't deserve any praise because praise belongs to him.

Daily hygiene in the first century usually involved anointing one's head and washing one's face. In other words, let your face be seen, and let it shine so as not to call attention to yourself, because unkempt hair and an unwashed face draw attention. He was saying, "Act like you're having a normal day so no one will know you're fasting."

Obviously, the hypocrites took their fasting a little too far. They didn't just want their friends to know; they wanted everybody in town to know. It is one thing to call a friend and say, "Please pray for me. I'm fasting for an answer from God today." It's a completely different thing to leave your house and go stand on a busy street corner with a sign that says, "Look at me, everyone! I'm fasting!" The former is a humble request; the latter is a prideful demand. The former is saying, "I'm searching for God"; the latter is saying, "Don't pay any attention to the Lord. Focus on me because I'm fasting!" A humble a person fasts in secret and looks for a reward from the Father. A prideful person fasts in public and looks for a reward through self-exaltation.

## PRIVATE FASTING, PUBLIC REWARDS

Jesus then instructed us to fast unto our Father. The hypocrites were fasting unto people because they made the fast public knowledge. The way to be sure your fast is unto your Father and not unto people is by keeping it a secret. "Thy Father which is in secret" means God is in the hidden place of your life; thus, consecrating in private is the way to get heavenly activity in the secret places of your life.

He then said, "Thy Father seeth in secret." Your Father notices things about you that no one else notices. He alone sees your sacrifice; therefore, you will never receive accolades and honor from everyone around you. Be assured, the amazing God you serve doesn't miss anything. He notices every detail of your efforts to please him. When you're on the floor at five in the morning weeping for the lost souls in your family, your neighbors don't know what you're doing. But you cry those tears because you believe God is there with you and within you in the secret place, and he will reward you with answers.

The most powerful reason we should fast privately is because private fasting brings public rewards. Jesus said, "If you fast in secret, your heavenly Father will reward you openly." Here is the revelation: If you fast in private, the reward will be public; if you fast in public, you've already received your reward, and it wasn't from God.

Thus, public rewards come from both kinds of fasting, and you determine the source of your reward. If you're fasting and everyone knows, the fast itself and the praise of others is your reward. People might think you're spiritual, but the reward they give you is merely their perception of who you are and what you've accomplished. However, if you fast in secret, the public won't see you as a hero, but they won't be able to deny the unending, undeserving, unexplainable hand of God on your life.

Most important, if your reward comes from man, it will be temporal. If man opens doors for you, man can close those doors. If people connect with you, they can disconnect with you. Why? Because the reward they give you is due to your pursuit of their affirmation. On the other hand, if your reward comes from God, the reward will be eternal. If God opens doors for you, man will never be able to close them. If God connects with you, man will never be able to disconnect you. It all depends on who you're fasting unto.

I can look back on some blessings I attained from previous fasts that I no longer retain because those rewards were from man. Doors that were opened are now closed because they were a temporary reward from man. In other words, I told too many people about my fast. Conversely, I also can look at rewards from fasting that are still alive and well because those rewards were an act of almighty God. Those rewards didn't come from man, so man can't take them away.

Another wonderful fact about fasting in secret is your strength on the fast will be provided by the one who dwells with you in secret. If you fast publicly, you will need to tell someone different every day to have strength that day to continue fasting. Telling a person may keep you fasting for that day, but there won't be any strength the next morning to go on unless you tell someone else. You depend on the compliments of others to endure another day of fasting.

Public fasting is, in many ways, addicting. People who fast publicly keep running out of temporal satisfaction, so they must search continually for it. However, if their source of strength is the Lord Jesus Christ, that brings lasting satisfaction. Humans can be used by the Lord to give that permanent strength, but only if the seeker is seeking the Lord first and foremost. God may then choose a human to bless the seeker with an impartation of strength that lasts.

## EVERLASTING FASTING

When fasting is done in secret unto the Lord, the rewards are everlasting. The word "everlasting" means "a long duration, forever." Several times in the scriptures you find the term "from everlasting to everlasting" when describing an attribute of the Lord. The God who rewards the fast completed in secret is one of everlasting attributes and everlasting covenants. The gifts and callings from God are without repentance, meaning he doesn't change his mind and take them back. He is the permanent rewarder. If he says, "Let there be light," then light will never stop being a reality unless he says, "Let there be darkness." Every word released from his mouth causes permanent change. Jesus Christ, according to Hebrews 13, is the same yesterday, today, and forever. He truly is the God from everlasting to everlasting.

## THE REWARDER

*But without faith it is impossible to please him: for he that cometh to God must believe that he is, and that he is a rewarder of them that diligently seek him.* (Heb. 11:6)

Fasting for an answer is displaying a much higher level of faith than just simply praying for that answer. Fasting is investing faith for a greater outcome than the reality one's flesh can project.

If faith is the mountain-mover, then fasting is the bulldozer that moves the granite boulders, hardened clay, and mammoth trees that make up that mountain. Unleashed faith in God is faith that demands answers. Stormy waves become solid ground when one steps out of a boat and into the atmosphere of faith. Faith will cause you to see a side of God that simply living for him will not let you see. Faith unleashed is ever moving forward. It's a game changer. No matter the diagnosis, if faith in God gets released into a situation, anything can change.

Faith gets answers because the word says God is pleased by faith. Conversely, any approach to God that is not faith-based is displeasing in his sight. I believe he is sickened when we approach him doubting his ability to intervene in the problem we're facing. We must believe he exists and that we will receive the reward if we diligently seek Him.

The Greek word "rewarder" is misthapodotes, meaning "the one who pays your wages." The rewarder becomes responsible for your provision because you always seek diligently after him. Seeking diligently means to crave, to demand, to require something back. God wants you to seek him, to crave him, to require his involvement in your life. God gets involved in your affairs only when you go to him with some type of request for divine intervention. The act of fasting is the deepest cry you can make for divine intervention. Then and only then can you see the attributes of a rewarding God fully manifested in your life on a permanent basis.

The rewarder wants you to believe that when you approach him with faith that he will pay your wages. No matter what type of wages those are, he has the resources to go above and beyond what any of us deserve. He can do "exceeding abundantly above all we can ask or think." Or, as the New International Version renders Ephesians 3:20, "Now to him who is able to do immeasurably more than all we ask or imagine, according to his power that is at work within us." The rewarder longs to be in control of your life. The million-dollar question is, will you let him?

Fasting is coming to God believing for the impossible because you know him to be your rewarder. The rewards of fasting go far beyond the rewards of feasting. The rewards of consecration burn to ashes the prior rewards of criticism. Anyone can know him as their rewarder—that is, anyone willing to diligently seek him.

We must ignite the flame of hunger for his involvement in our lives by fasting. Fasting is like the lighter fluid that sets the wood ablaze. The wood is dead and dry before the fluid saturates it. Once lighter fluid is poured over a dry log, branch, or twig, there is now an expectation that fire will erupt once the match touches it. The match or the lighter is the prayer that goes up after the fluid of fasting has touched the wood or the need. Instantaneous combustion is the result. Are you ready for God to make things explode in your favor?

Prayer combined with fasting is the most explosive combination for getting fire to fall. The fire falls where there is a sacrifice and an altar. If you tie a sacrificial offering (in the form of a fast) on top of the altar you have built by prayer, you can expect the consuming fire of God's glory to fall and dominate the once empty altar. His fire searches for altars built through prayer and covered by the sacrifice of a fast.

## THIRSTY FIRE

The fire from God shot down out of heaven, consuming Elijah's sacrifice, the wood, the stones of the altar, and the dust. It even "licked up" the water in the trench Elijah had dug. The fire was—literally—thirsty. God's fire not only is hungry for our sacrifice, but it also is thirsty for the water of faith to be poured out in expectation. Elijah had so much faith in the God of fire that after he had built the altar, arranged the wood, and topped it with the sacrifice, he drenched everything with twelve barrels of water. It was so much water that it filled the trench he had dug around the perimeter of the altar. He knew if his sacrifice warranted God's attention, God would, in response, consume his sacrifice and everything around it. In other words, Elijah knew the fire of God wasn't just hungry; it was thirsty too. Faith quenches God's thirst.

Is there anything extra you can pour over your sacrifice in expectation that God will do the miraculous in your life? If the fire falls upon your sacrifice, will its thirst be quenched after it consumes your offering? Or will the trenches around your altar still be full of water? Is your fast dripping with faith? I hope so! The rewarder is about to send fire. Make sure your sacrifice has been soaked with expectation.

## RAIN IS COMING

I find it amazing that Elijah's helpers were able to find enough water to fill twelve barrels, because the country had been in the throes of a drought for three and a half years. Maybe there was a natural spring trickling out of the side of Mount Carmel. Maybe the helpers dipped the barrels of water out of a cistern that had been dug to preserve the precious water. Or maybe the helpers descended the mountain to the shores of the Mediterranean Sea, filled the barrels, and schlepped them back up to the summit. Wherever or however they obtained the water, as soon as the fire licked up Elijah's offering, God told Elijah to inform the king that there was a sound of abundance of rain. In other words, the answer was imminent; the drought was over; revival was on the horizon!

God will never give you an IOU. After drinking the water, God unleashed the greatest rainstorm of their lives. Could it be that God was simply waiting for an altar, a sacrifice, and some water so he could send them their answer? How close are you to the arrival of your long-awaited answers? Is it possible that answer is hungry or thirsty? Does God need you to build an altar of prayer, go on a sacrificial fast, and then drench it with faith? I challenge you to find out.

## THE SOUND OF ABUNDANCE

Elijah heard the rumbling and whooshing of the approaching storm. It was the sound of the abundance of rain. The Hebrew word for "sound" is qowl, meaning voice. "Abundance" in the Hebrew is hamown, meaning roar, sound, crowd, great number, multitude, wealth. I believe Elijah heard the roar of a great multitude and the voice of wealth approaching in the form of rain.

## CHAPTER 9

# The Glorious Climb

After Moses' first forty-day fast, he descended Mount Sinai carrying the Ten Commandments only to be confronted by a shocking scene. The people whom God had called him to lead out of Egypt and into the Promised Land, the people whom he had proven himself to, prayed over, instructed, and risked his life to lead out of Egypt, were dancing naked, worshiping a golden calf. They had replaced Jehovah with a golden idol. They also had replaced their God-sent leader with Aaron, because, as they said, Moses had been on the mountain so long. "We don't know what happened to this fellow Moses, who brought us up here from the land of Egypt" (Exod. 32:1, NLT). They somehow had persuaded Aaron to melt down their collection of golden jewelry and mold it into the form of a calf, possibly a representation of the gods of Egypt. When people desire to sin, the two voices they want separation from are the Lord and their spiritual leader.

Can you imagine being in the mountaintop alone with God, being given commandments that were supposed to guide the people in godly living, and then descending the mountain only to encounter an erotic, evil atmosphere? It is scary to realize how close the Lord God was as the people were reveling in their folly. They had polluted and perverted not only their miraculous deliverance, but the Lord's grand plan for creating a godly nation and the blessings he had bestowed upon them. They were heedless of his presence. I cannot imagine the anger that boiled in Moses' veins as he approached their wicked orgy.

Moses' immediate reaction was not, as you may think, one of carnality; rather, it was one of righteous indignation and overwhelming frustration. It was similar to the indignation Jesus felt when he walked into the temple and saw the moneychangers, whom, everyone knew, took advantage of the people by overcharging for the birds and animals they bought for their sacrifices. Jesus shouted, "'My Temple will be called a house of prayer,' but you have turned it into a den of thieves!" (Matt. 21:13, NLT). He scattered their coins all over the floor, turned over their tables, and drove the moneychangers and their animals out of the temple.

Moses' reaction was no less violent. When he witnessed the lurid calf worship, he threw down the priceless tablets of stone containing the commandments written by the finger of God, and the stones shattered into pieces. Maybe the chaotic scene triggered thoughts of things he had been through on behalf of these people: his initial reluctance followed by his decision to fulfill his role as deliverer, the courage it took to face the Hebrew slaves and persuade them of God's mindfulness and of his plan for their deliverance, his frustration at Pharaoh for continually changing his mind and hardening his heart, his leading the people across the Red Sea amidst the frightening walls of water standing on each side, his longsuffering with the people's constant murmuring against him and against God:

1. They blamed Moses for making their lives harder after Pharaoh demanded that they collect their own straw.

2. They panicked when they saw Pharaoh's army pursuing and accused, "Moses, you brought us out here to die!"

3. After marching for three days without water, they finally found some, but it was undrinkable, and they said it was Moses's fault.

4. On their way to Sinai the people murmured against Moses and longed for the food they had enjoyed in Egypt.

5. They chided with Moses because they were thirsty.

Whatever his reasoning, Moses lost it. He had just spent forty days communing with his creator but found himself back in the flesh (carnal nature) only a few seconds after observing the people's revelry. Crazy people can make you feel crazy sometimes. I am sure if Moses could do it over again, he would have set the commandments aside and thrown something else to show his displeasure.

## PREVIOUS CONSECRATIONS AREN'T ENOUGH

After some serious cleansing of the camp that involved the destruction of the golden calf and the revelers who had worshiped it, Moses had a reality check. Even though he had cleared away the residue of evil in the camp, he knew he had left something on the mountain. Questions must have been coursing through his mind: "How could I have been so peaceful in Jehovah's presence and so angry as soon as I left? Did I do wrong? Did I lose something between the mountaintop and the camp? I fasted forty days on that mountaintop, so how could the effects of such a powerful encounter with God fade so quickly? Did I fail to receive something God was trying to instill in me?" Moses sensed there was more for him on the mountaintop than two tablets of stone with commandments written on them.

We cannot depend on yesterday's sacrifices to carry us through our current battles. I believe that fasting brings favor in our future, but I also believe it is dangerous to assume that because we once walked with God or that we once had a great encounter with the Lord that we are now free to react to the actions of others in any way we desire. Too many people are enjoying today the rewards of yesterday's consecrations while not hungering for more.

If we assume the rewards we're enjoying now because of yesterday's victories in prayer and fasting are permanent, and we no longer have to pursue the Lord with that level of passion, we are deceived. Rewards and favor are not a sign of current righteousness but rather a sign of past righteousness. Righteousness means to please God, and people who please God always receive rewards. However, it is scary when we presume that past righteousness is alive today in our spirit despite of our fleshly activities.

Help us, Lord, to stop feasting on our past accomplishments in the Spirit and begin to pray with a fervent hunger that cannot be quenched. Moses cried out to the Lord, "Show me your glory!" He realized that his angry reaction revealed a lack of glory in his life. "Lord, I need more now than what I received before!" Let that be someone's cry right now.

## CLIMB THE MOUNTAIN AGAIN

There was a problem with Moses' request to see the glory of the Lord. The problem wasn't eligibility on Moses' behalf; rather, it was the location from which he requested to see the glory. The problem with big prayers being answered is rarely eligibility on the seeker's behalf, but rather the determining factors are usually timing, location, and the ultimate will and purpose of God. Your prayer request might be right, but the timing might be wrong. Maybe what you are asking cannot happen until some growth in your life takes place.

Moses asked to see the glory while he was still in the camp, surrounded by people who seemingly had no desire to see any such thing. They had committed the great sin of worshiping the golden calf, and the Lord sent a plague as punishment. The Lord then told Moses he would not be accompanying them when they entered the Promised Land. Moses went to the Tent of Meeting and pleaded with the Lord to forgive the people—reminding him they were God's people, not Moses' people. After Moses' fervent prayer, God consented to go with them as they entered the Promised Land. That's when Moses asked to see God's glory.

The Lord informed him that granting his request would involve another climb up the sacred mountain. Granted, he could hear the voice of God in the camp, but if he wanted to see God's glory, he would have to be at a higher elevation. Some things can happen only on the mountaintop. Some rewards can manifest only after you've climbed out of the comfort zone of mediocrity and apathy and forced your flesh to endure the pain of sacrifice. "Moses, if you want to see my glory, there's a mountain in the way."

Moses had to climb the mountain again if he wanted to experience this glorious encounter. Furthermore, this second climb would be much harder than the first. This time he wouldn't begin the ascent empty handed and receive the ready-made tablets of stone at the summit. This time it wouldn't be God hewing the tablets of stone out of the mountain; it would be Moses. Then, since God had forbidden anyone to accompany him, he had to carry those heavy stones up himself. This second climb would involve a lot more sweat.

Sometimes God makes us earn the answers we want by asking us to bring a greater sacrifice than what we've offered before. The greater the sacrifice, the more appreciative we will be of the reward. "Moses, you won't be so quick to throw those stones on the ground because you worked so hard hewing them out of the mountain and carrying them up to the summit."

If, in the past, you have thrown away your ministry, calling, or encounters with God, please hear me: There is still hope for you! You are not finished; you just have to carry a heavier load this time. Make up your mind that you're going to ascend the mountain of consecration and that you're willing to carry whatever load you are required to carry to get back to where the glory dwells.

## CUT, CARRY, CLIMB

Moses was going to get the workout of a lifetime to start this second fast. First, he was commanded to hew out the stone tablets. Chiseling stones in the desert with no food or water on day one of his fast had to have been miserable. Sometimes God expects you to cut some things out as you begin your climb into his glory. The rocks you are carrying are going to be written on by the hand of God, because this encounter will be greater than your mind can retain all at once. God wants to write down everything that happens in this encounter. He will etch it into your life, leaving you forever changed.

Logic says it is harder to carry those heavy rocks up a mountain than it would be to climb unencumbered. It would be easier to wait until you get to the summit to chisel the stones out of the mountain. But Moses didn't hesitate to obey God's command that the tablets had to be cut before the climb. He knew the honor of the mountaintop invitation from Jehovah, and he was not about to do anything incorrectly this time. Expectation consumed him as he chiseled out the stones. God was going to show him something neither he nor anyone else had never seen before! He was coming to talk to him in person. Was the added burden of the climb going to be worth it? Was he actually going to make it to the top? The questions had to have been coming at a rapid pace.

Moses didn't have boots specially designed for mountain climbing. He had to carry those heavy rocks while toiling up the rough terrain in sandals. What if frustration would have hit at some point during the climb? What if his foot had slipped on some loose rock? What if he had dropped the stones accidentally and they plummeted down the mountainside, exploding on rugged crags? Moses never complained, though, for this was an opportunity of a lifetime!

This is how you must see the fast if you're going to finish it. Instead of dreading the fast (probably resulting in ending it prematurely), anticipate it. Get excited! The king wants an appointment with you. He wants to change your world. The weights you're carrying aren't excess baggage. Those heavy burdens aren't unnecessary frustrations. They are the pages of your book that God wants to write on.

Remember when the four men carried the lame man to see Jesus? They couldn't enter the house where Jesus was teaching because the crowd had filled the building and was spilling out the doorway. If their friend was going to receive a miracle, it wasn't going to be easy because no one was moving out of the way to let them get to the master. (The lesson here is that if you want the greatest of encounters with the Lord, don't take the route that is crowded by others.) The four men had only one option when it came to getting their sick friend to Jesus: they had to climb. To be more specific, they had to climb and carry.

Typical of many first-century homes, there was a staircase on the back of the house that led to the rooftop. The rooftop consisted of a gridwork of wooden trusses crisscrossed with thick straw mats that were smeared over with clay. Rooftops saw daily use for storing tools, drying clothes, and gathering to catch the evening breezes. In short, they were like an unenclosed extra room. The four men stood looking up at the narrow flight of stone stairs, wondering if they were strong enough to carry their friend to the top. Would they then be able to cut through the trusses, the straw matting, and the clay that had hardened as it baked in the relentless Palestinian sun? There it was again: cut, carry, climb.

The four men could have told their crippled friend, "Sorry, we tried. But there are too many people blocking the way and they won't let us through." But no, they made up their mind that they would climb over any obstacle. This was their moment. Sometimes you have to declare, "This is going to be my moment! If people try to stop me from getting to Jesus on this fast, I'm going to climb up some other way. If I can't get through the door, I'll take the stairs!"

Once they accepted the challenge, they knew they had to keep going. They had come too far to stop now. "C'mon, fellas. We've got to hurry because Jesus might be done teaching soon. Simon, rummage around up here for some rope. The rest of us, let's get busy cutting through this roof." They cut and tore through the thick layers until the roof was open, then they lowered their sick friend to the floor right in front of Jesus. They had made it to the miracle moment! Jesus immediately forgave the lame man's sins and then raised him up. Sometimes Jesus waits on us to cut, carry, and climb, and then he will do the rest.

## PRESENT YOURSELF TO GOD

Moses finished hewing out the rocks and chiseling them smooth. The moment to start his climb was finally here. He had made it to the foot of the mountain and his fast had begun. There is something hidden in the conversation between God and Moses that was the driving force and the motivation for Moses to conquer that mountain the next morning. No, it wasn't the Ten Commandments. It was a statement had God made:

> *And be ready in the morning, and come up in the morning unto mount Sinai, and present thyself there to me in the top of the mount.* (Exod. 34:2)

God did not say, "Present the tablets of stone unto me for inspection." He did not say, "Present your case to me" or "What can I do for you since you've worked so hard to come up here?" He said, "Present yourself there to me." The stone tablets were just part of the appointment. The real reason and motivation for this second climb and this second fast was the promise that he would see the glory of God.

Moses had to pass three tests to prove he was in the spirit and thus wouldn't fail this time. The first test was one of submission: cut, carry, and climb. The second test was one of consecration: fasting forty days a second time. (While it is not mentioned that he was ever commanded to fast, Moses knew enough about the holiness of God not to dare approach him without it. The less food, the less flesh.) The third test was one of presentation: he was to stand before God.

## ALL RISE!

An even better way of understanding the command to present oneself is seeing it from a courtroom perspective. After all, God is the lawgiver, the judge, and the jury. Whenever a judge enters a courtroom the bailiff will announce, "All rise!" Everyone in the courtroom must stand to their feet in reverence for the judge. If someone doesn't stand, they are not allowed to stay. Since no one was on the mountaintop to serve as bailiff to announce God's arrival, he became his own bailiff. He said, "When I am there, you will stand."

As you are fasting, remember God is the judge. Don't present yourself and start making demands; rather, present yourself with humility and thanksgiving at his arrival. He doesn't have to meet with you, but because he loves you so much, he, at times, graces you with his manifested presence. What an honor to stand before the king, the judge of all eternity, and present yourself before him in the sacred consecration of fasting!

Fasting will bring one into the presence of the Lord much quicker than any other type of consecration. The Bible is full of stories that prove that when nothing else will get an answer, fasting will. It is the entryway into the courtroom of the Most High.

Someone must have taught Esther the value of fasting, for, when she and her people were under a death sentence, she knew if there was any hope of deliverance, she had to present herself to the king. The only problem was, she wasn't allowed into the inner court of the palace where the king was sitting on his throne. Her decision to fast for three days without food or water proved to be the exact key to finding favor with the king, for on the third day when she approached his majesty, no doubt weak in the knees, she was granted access to any request she wanted. This ultimately led to the rescue of her people.

Had Esther taken the easier path of simply waiting on God to move in her people's behalf, the story could have ended much differently. Instead, she made a stand and presented herself—and you can too! Are you facing a dilemma that seems unfixable? Are you out of options? Are you running short of grace? Is your back up against the wall and you don't know where to turn? Are you stuck in a rut and can't pray your way out? You need to try fasting. It is going to shock you what God will do for you upon the completion of your sacrifice of consecration.

## THE JUDGE CHANGED HIS MIND

I'm adding this next story to show you that fasting can bring rewards even when the odds are stacked against you. A friend of mine once informed me that he and his wife were in a bitter custody battle with her ex-husband for two of her children. The judge had previously awarded the children to the ex-husband due to financial problems on the lady's part. As soon as he was awarded the children, the ex-husband informed the children's mother that they were no longer allowed to go church or to even mention church or God, and they weren't allowed to have a Bible. The mother continued to fight for her babies, who desperately wanted to be with her and go to church again.

Court date after court date she would come back home with the bad news that her ex-husband still had custody. As the time approached for one last court appearance, her new husband, my friend and a great man of God, asked me what they should do. I answered immediately: he had to go on a fast. He felt prompted to fast for ten days before the court date and completed the ten days full of faith. The night before the hearing, he texted me, asking for prayer, and I told him I would pray. I was across the country preaching a revival but would do my best to bring the need before the Lord.

That next day, I am ashamed to say, I forgot to bring up his need during my prayer time. Later in the afternoon, quite some time after the scheduled court appearance, I remembered the situation. I felt terrible and asked the Lord to forgive me for forgetting to cover the hearing in prayer. I also figured things must not have gone well, for I surely would have heard from him by then had there been any change in the decision. Still, I felt the Lord prompting me to intercede, so I texted my friend that I was going to pray. His response was, "Perfect timing! The judge just went into his chambers to decide who gets the children."

When I saw that text, faith blitzed me and I fell to my knees, believing God for a miracle. I sent one more text, asking my friend the name of the judge, and when he answered, I began asking the Lord to remember my friend's ten-day fast and send angels into that judge's chambers to influence his decision. You have to believe that God is rooting for you when you're fasting for a miracle!

The phone rang about an hour later, and caller ID announced my friend's name. I picked it up and heard him say, "Bro, when we got to the court today our own attorney said we needed a miracle." He then stated that the judge's last words before entering his chambers to make the decision was that he saw no need to change anything in the current situation because there wasn't enough evidence for a reversal in the ruling. But when the judge came out of his chambers, he said he had "changed his mind," reversed the ruling, and was awarding the children back to the mother. That shows the power of fasting! Even a judge cannot resist the cry of a fasting spirit that longs for an answer. The children now safely abide with the mother and my friend, her husband.

## ENTER THE GLORY

As I mentioned in the introduction, Moses entered the glory on this second fast and had one of the greatest encounters with God any human has ever had. God showed him his "hinder parts" or better stated, his back. I (as well as many Bible scholars) believe this is the place and time where God showed Moses his creative acts, and Moses later recorded the events in the book of Genesis.

God also renewed a covenant with Moses on the mountaintop. The lesson to be learned here is simply if you will consecrate, cut, carry, and climb, God will create a covenant with you. God has something for you at the end of your long fast that will be worth the climb! Moses was in the glory of God for forty days without food or water, and it was worth it.

Moses' experience teaches us that when we are near the glory of God, we become like a sponge. God's glory permeated Moses' face until it shone like the sun. When he descended the mountain, his face was too bright to look upon and he had to wear a veil to cover up the brightness of the glory that had permeated his being. He didn't need to tell everyone he had been with the Lord; they could tell just by looking at him. Fasting can change the way others perceive you. Something about you has changed. You could call it transfiguration.

## TRANSFIGURATION COMES THROUGH FASTING

Over a thousand years after Moses' death, Jesus took three disciples to the top of the mount of transfiguration. On that mountaintop Moses and Elijah appeared and conversed with Jesus. According to the biblical account, these two were the only other people besides Jesus to fast forty days. Jesus' countenance was bright like the sun, for God's glory was being revealed. The same glory that once had lit up the face of Moses was now shining through Jesus, and Moses was there to see it. There is a place in God where you always stay near the glory. Fasting takes you to that place.

Fasting for the Lord for extended periods of time not only will change how others see you, it will cause them to seek out what you have already found. They knew the "old you," but now you're different. Now you're tuned in to another world. Now you have a glow about your life and they know you have been in the secret place of the Most High. You have been transfigured. So climb, my friend. It's a glorious climb!

◆◇————————●————————◇◆

## CHAPTER 10

## Ships in the Deep

*They that go down to the sea in ships, that do business in great waters; these see the works of the Lord, and his wonders in the deep.* (Ps. 107:23–24)

How do I go deeper? How do I get to the places in God that I've only heard of or read about? I hear questions like these all the time. In fact, I've asked myself the same questions. In this chapter I want to take you on a three-day journey I had with the Lord, during which he answered these and other questions. I hope this helps someone.

We must accept a process from the Lord if we desire to dwell in the deep. We don't just get saved and then go swimming in the ocean depths of God. There is a journey of growth we all must take to get to these destinations. There must also be a hunger for the deeper things. Too many people are satisfied just getting saved; they have no desire for the things that are available if they would just invest some sacrifice and desire. If the previous sentence describes you, then this chapter is not for you.

## FOUR WAYS TO GET HUNGRY

On my three-day journey with the Lord, the first thing he told me was if I wanted to go deeper, I had to increase my spiritual hunger. Individuals cannot increase their spiritual hunger if they don't first know how to develop spiritual hunger. He showed me four things every child of God can do to develop that hunger.

First, develop spiritual habits that challenge you. Go beyond your devotions. If your morning ritual is to wake up at 6:00 a.m. every day, get a cup of coffee, read a page in your Bible and then whisper a thirty-second prayer on your way out the door, that is not sacrifice; that is routine. If it does not challenge you, it will not change you.

If you desire to go deeper, your devotions must be challenging. Therefore, transform your devotions into consecrations. That is the best way I can describe it. Take the routine and add the ingredient of challenge. The word, prayer, and fasting are three immediate things that should come to mind. Increase your daily Bible reading. (Side note: B.R.E.A.D programs are fine, but they will not challenge you.) Pray longer than thirty seconds. Fast more than a mid-morning after-breakfast snack. You can do it! Challenge your devotions. Tell yourself to get a greater hunger for his word.

Second, learn to apply these consecrations long term. Anyone can go on a God splurge for a few days, but the soldiers who are still standing at the end of the war are those who transformed their temporary sacrifice into a consecrated lifestyle. Find the place in him where you aren't satisfied with a momentary encounter due to a brief desire for him, but rather a never-ending hunger to go deeper into his presence. It is possible to become engulfed in God's presence by thinking about ways to capture his attention.

Write down the consecrations so you can read them daily and dwell on them throughout each day. If you will transform your sacrifice into a consecrated life, one year from now (if the Lord tarries) your life will be quite different.

Third, talk to someone who is hungrier for God than you are, because their great hunger for the Lord is contagious. I've never been around someone who craved God's attention without it affecting me. There is something about this type of person that causes me to want to go deeper. When someone who is consumed with growing in the Lord starts talking to you, their words will ignite a dormant fire in your soul. You will feel challenged, and you will feel desire rising in you to join in the pursuit. Hunger is a consuming fire that is constantly searching for others to impact and contact.

Finally, read the books, listen to the voices, and watch the warriors that dwell in deeper waters than yourself. You might be wondering how you will know when someone has delved deeper in God than you. I've found three simple ways to find out.

First, their life and even the sound of their voice will convict you. When someone has a presence that brings conviction to you, it is a signal they have been swimming in deeper waters. You need the voice of conviction to be near if there is going to be increased consecration. Don't let your flesh lie to you and convince you that you can be consecrated without conviction.

Second, the person in deeper waters will have a walk with God that will make you hungry for more. If just being around someone makes you want to go pray, then you know they are swimming in deeper waters. For instance, anytime my wife and I are around Joy Haney, the great intercessor and author for so many decades, we feel like she has just come out of a fervent prayer meeting to talk to us.

Third, the person who dwells in deeper waters will draw respect from you with their wisdom and experiences. Reverence for their walk and their wisdom will come upon you. When you're around this person, something in you whispers to be silent and glean from their battles or from their very presence. If the phone rings and you see his or her name, answer the call no matter where you are. This feeling is a blessing from the Lord coming to you in the form of an encounter with greatness.

Each time someone of this magnitude connects with you on any level, it probably is a test to see if you're interested in growing beyond where you currently are. The person that draws the respect from you most likely won't realize they are being used as a vessel to test you, because the test has been sent from the Lord. In other words, it is like a ship passing you in the night on its way to deeper waters, and you get to witness the encounter. The encounter, however, has a question attached to it each time. Usually that question is, "Do you want to go deeper?" Never underestimate prayers, conversations, phone calls, texts, or emails from people who are moving like ships in the deep. There aren't very many of them out there anymore, so wait with expectation. After all, when the student is ready, the teacher will appear.

## BE A SHIP, NOT A CANOE

If you desire to be like a seagoing vessel and voyage across the ocean deeps, it is imperative that in your walk with God you desire to be a vessel unto honor, as described by Paul. Be a vessel God can take into any place at any time.

In other words, be a ship, not a canoe. Ships can handle the roughest of winds and waves, but canoes can capsize with the slightest resistance. On a ship, you can walk, run, and jump and the ship will not alter its course. If you try those things on a canoe, I hope you know how to swim. One wrong move on a canoe and the journey is over. Desire to be a vessel that can fight your way through the roughest of storms or the deepest of seas. Ask the Lord to take you into places you've only heard about. I believe that what you're going through right now is God building in you a seaworthiness for deeper waters. God is upgrading you from a canoe in the river to a war ship in the ocean. Great things are coming, so don't fail the training!

Ships require a far greater inventory for their voyage than smaller vessels. From the anchors to the ballast, from the radios to the flares, from the fire extinguishers to the life vests, there is a weighty load for the ship to carry on each endeavor. It doesn't matter if it is a cruise ship or a war ship; the load adds up to a staggering number of tons. If you want to venture into deeper waters, you must be willing to carry a heavy load. If everything has to be perfect in your world before you will pray or fast, you aren't a ship yet. The load you carry, although stressful at times, holds within it the virtues given to you to survive sailing through the deep. What often weighs you down is actually the anchor you will need if the current becomes too strong or the waves too boisterous.

If you are under a heavy load that you feel is handicapping your potential, learn to use the load as your fuel. The load you don't want to bear any more needs to meet the "you" that knows how to say, "I was built for this." Others might not be able to carry this load (or should I say this cross), but you were made for this moment.

Remember when Esther's fast saved her people? She stepped into that fast with a word from the Lord that was spoken through her cousin Mordecai. He said her captive people whom she desperately cared for were going to be set free by someone; whether it would be her or someone else remained to be seen. Mordecai said if she didn't follow through, God would turn to a different source to effect deliverance for his people. He then uttered the most motivating statement she would ever hear in her lifetime: "Who knoweth whether thou art come to the kingdom for such a time as this?" (Esther 4:14).

In other words, "Esther, it's time to go big or go home. This load of worry you're carrying needs to be transformed into a fast full of faith for your answer." The answer will come to someone who assesses the weight of the circumstance and decides to step out of doubting flesh and into the spirit of faith. God will help you once he sees you aren't going to quit just because the load is heavy. Remember who you are and whose you are. Never settle for the mediocrity of paddling around in a pond when you are destined for the ocean. Be a ship, not a canoe.

## HOW TO LAUNCH

Launching into the depths of consecration requires several actions on your part as a believer. You must first humble your soul by developing a consistent prayer life. Don't expect the Lord to allow you to fast very long if you never pray. The spirit world will chew you up and spit you out—or your own pride will consume you. One of the most powerful scriptures on what to expect next in your life is found in Proverbs:

> *Before destruction the heart of man is haughty, and before honor is humility.* (Prov. 18:12)

This verse says it all. You can tell what is about to happen in your life by the manner in which your heart presents itself. If your heart is haughty (high or exalted), you can expect a crash around the corner. However, if you are working at humbling yourself daily, you can expect the favor of God to sweep in.

It is vital that you develop a consistent prayer life. It is like untying the rope that keeps you moored to the dock of carnality. Living in daily communication with your creator allows you to delve into deeper currents. Early-morning prayer is an even more diligent attempt on the believer's part to launch out into the deep. Rising before the sun to receive your assignment sends a signal into the depths that you are launching out that day. Early-morning prayer declares, "Today, I will be led by the Spirit."

If early-morning prayer is casting off from the dock, then fasting is most definitely the undercurrent that draws you into the deep. It is the invisible force under the surface of your life that causes you to hear, see, and live the dreams that can appear only to the consecrated. Fasting causes movement in the Spirit. It causes the vessel to move into unchartered waters and experience the wonders of the deep.

## SECRETS TO DWELLING IN THE DEEP

It is one thing to enter deep waters; it is quite another thing to dwell in deep waters. When a ship launches out from shore, it takes a while to reach the deepest of waters; it usually is a slow process. However, if the ship sails far enough out to sea, the ocean will hide the ship from viewers standing on the shore. In other words, your vessel must become hidden in the deep if your intend to last in the deep. Following are three attributes that are essential for living in the deep waters of the Spirit.

1. Humility. If everyone can see you, you aren't far enough from the shore. Humility is the submarine of spiritual warfare,

and it must become a primary focus to a hungry vessel desiring more. Humility hides you in the currents of the Spirit and preserves you in the ocean of his purpose.

One of the quickest ways to reverse course and head back to shallow waters is to become competitive with other vessels in the deep. Competition is often the silent killer of deep ministries that do not last. A powerful way to kill the spirit of competition is through connection. And if connection kills competition, it follows that competition kills connection. I'll sort out that mouthful by saying you probably won't compete with someone with whom you feel connected or united. Conversely, you might compete with someone with whom you feel no connection.

2. Outward focus. A mission-minded child of God usually will be focused on being a blessing to others and not opposing them in jealousy. It is vital that you keep your daily consecration alive so you won't change from being a war ship to being a cruise ship. You aren't in the depths to enjoy the buffets; you're there to do your part in the war for humanity. You must see the lost saved at any cost.

3. Tenacity. A person who is tenacious is extremely persistent in adhering to or doing something. Just because you've earned your way into the deep waters of revelation with past consecrations does not mean you can dwell there in carnality. The vessel must continually be searching to go deeper. Paul told us that he died daily. He took nothing for granted and neither should you. You must endeavor to never stop seeking the face of God.

## GROWING WHILE GOING

The quickest way into the deep is also the slowest way into the deep. I meet a lot of people who want a crash course on accessing the deep things of God but have no real interest in participating in the full process of growth. If there ever was a spiritual microwave mentality that consumes a generation, it is this generation. Some assume that if they pray fifteen minutes and fast breakfast that they deserve a ministry like John the Baptist. Why would anyone want to skip the full experience? It is time to embrace the process of growth and realize that almost every growth lesson involves taking time to develop. The Lord is merciful to his children in that he protects us from seeing too much too quickly. Growing in the Lord on a daily, consistent basis and ever seeking his presence is the proper way to plunge into deeper revelations about him and more intimate encounters with him. Grow into the deep. Take your time. Always be a student and fast whenever you can.

## FASTING WITH FAITH

You can go only so far in the kingdom of God without fasting. Yes, I believe in "feasting" and believing, but I also believe in "fasting" and believing. Verbal Bean once stated that he didn't feel the need to pray as often while fasting, and he prayed a lot! He said that he had that much faith in the fasting he was doing. I concur. It is more difficult to have fervent prayer on a long fast than it is to have fervent prayer when the body is eating food. I also believe that if you launch an extended fast with a war ship load of faith, you will see results from that fast that you could not attain through any prayer meeting.

There is something about fasting with faith that brings you closer to the Lord. I truly believe that I will receive what I have the faith to fast for. I also believe that if I am praying with faith for something before fasting and it is not being answered, then the answer is not necessarily no, but rather the answer lies in a fast that can break open the gate. You must enter an extended fast with full confidence that you're going to get the answer you're searching for. God honors that type of faith. I use the terms "praying faith" and "fasting faith."

A person praying with desperation and emotion is sincere in their search for the answer, but fasting numbs the feelings and emotions and boosts sincerity to a higher level than a person can reach through prayer alone. You might not feel like you are getting any closer to the Lord or his favor during the fast, but ignore those feelings. You have never been more serious, more focused, and more desperate than when you're on a fast. Your flesh is losing control of the outcome that lies ahead, and the Lord is watching you with favor in his eyes. Don't beat yourself up while on a fast if you can't feel anything that day in prayer. Have faith in your fast, not your feelings. Have faith in God, not your emotions!

The longer the fast, the greater your faith needs to be for receiving specific answers. I believe that when it comes to receiving answers and favor from God, nothing can replace fasting. I know when I'm getting serious about an answer that I need if I fast about it. Fasting about a previous prayer request is like saying, "I'm more serious now, Lord." Fasting is telling the Lord how important your previous requests in prayer are to you. It is also removing the fleshly pride inside of you (that wishes to take the glory for the answer) because you now know that unless you die on the altar of a fast, you will not get the answer. Your life will never be the same once you add the element of faith to fasting. People who attempt fasting without faith usually don't get their answer. Be specific with the Lord and believe that you will get your answer.

The ship is you, the engine is prayer, the undercurrent is fasting, and the fuel is faith. Be a vessel that prays consistently, fasts frequently, and is constantly full of faith. The deep waters are awaiting your arrival.

## CHAPTER 11

# The Secrets About Strongholds

*(For the weapons of our warfare are not carnal, but mighty through God to the pulling down of strong holds;) casting down imaginations, and every high thing that exalteth itself against the knowledge of God, and bringing into captivity every thought to the obedience of Christ; and having in a readiness to revenge all disobedience, when your obedience is fulfilled.* (2 Cor. 10:4–6)

This chapter is the result of a statement made to me by my pastor, Brian Kinsey, concerning a person's thought life. He said, "The enemy's strongholds in people's lives develop through breaches created by something that has happened in their life." When he said that to me, my mind began pursuing this revelation, and now I have the privilege of passing it on to you. Are you ready to pull down your strongholds?

Weapons in the spirit world are not bombs, missiles, and guns; they are words. The world we live in was made by the word of the Lord. He spoke, and things manifested. Words are so important in the heavens that when the archangel Michael fought the devil, Lucifer, for the body of Moses, the war was a word war. Words carry weight, and both heaven and hell desire to be magnified by the words of our mouths.

When Satan came to Jesus at the end of his fast, tempting him to turn stones into bread, Jesus said, "Man shall not live by bread alone, but by every word that proceedeth out of the mouth of God." Words can bring life, and words can bring death. Words can enable, and words can disable. Words have the power to produce confidence, and words have the ability to produce condemnation. Words can stir faith, and words can cause fear.

Our words are products of our thoughts. Matthew wrote, "Out of the abundance of the heart the mouth speaketh" (12:34). What lives within us ultimately comes out of us. Words are weapons that can be used to magnify either heaven or hell. When our words are Spirit led, they edify others; when our words are driven by the flesh, or carnal, we tend to push others down.

Our weapons are not carnal but mighty through God to the pulling down of strongholds. Our words work best when they are led by the Spirit of God. However, if we are not being led by the Spirit, our words will reveal strongholds in our personal lives.

Before we discuss where the strongholds of the enemy are located, let us discover what a stronghold is. "Stronghold" in the original Greek is the word ochyroma, meaning a castle or a fortress. When you hear someone preach about a stronghold the enemy has in someone's life, it means the enemy is building a castle or a fortress in this person's world. If you have ever prayed for the Lord to bring down strongholds in your church or your family, you were praying that the Lord would invade the fortresses of hell.

What is even more troublesome to me than the fact that hell is trying to build these castles in people's lives is discovering the location of these fortresses. The word of God reveals the locations where these strongholds are being built. (See 2 Cor. 10:4–6 above.) Clearly, the enemy is building castles in our minds through our thoughts. Thoughts can come to us from the enemy, and we can either rebuke them and make them leave or we can allow them to remain and begin building the fortress of hell within. The breach in our defense that was opened up through trial or trauma now becomes the pathway through which hell gains entrance into our mind.

As I pondered the passage in 2 Corinthians 10, I began to see how a thought can become a "high thing." In the Greek a "high thing" means something elevated. Paul was using the term to describe thoughts that come from the enemy and oppose the knowledge of God in a person's life. If these thoughts go unchallenged, they will take up residence in a person's mind, and before the person knows it, these thoughts will begin to elevate. Before long, what was once a whisper of hell becomes a wrecking ball inside the castle (stronghold) in the person's mind, all because the thought went unrebuked.

A panic attack, for instance, is simply a thought that morphed into a high thing by being allowed to stay in one's mind. An angry outburst can be traced back to a thought that, when dwelt upon instead of dealt with, gathered strength. The longer it was allowed to stay, the more the stronghold was fortified. Research shows that harmful addictions can be traced back to the thought life, because, if the whisper is granted access, it immediately begins to build a seemingly indestructible fortress.

The word of God instructs that we are to bring into captivity every thought to the obedience of Christ. In the Greek, "bringing into captivity" means to lead away captive. It is the will of God for us to check thoughts at the door of our mind before we grant them access into our spirit. I believe God wants you to arrest the things that are trying to trespass into your life via your thoughts. God won't arrest your thoughts for you; it's up to you to intentionally halt the thoughts that come to you until you find out which kingdom they came from. Obviously, most of your thoughts come neither from heaven or hell, but spiritual sensitivity and wisdom should alert you when destructive thoughts come into your mind.

If you've ignored a destructive thought and allowed it to take up residence in your mind, that thought cannot simply be rebuked and then dissolved; it must be repented over if it is to be removed. Repentance requests God's intervention in a situation that you yourself can't change. Again, if the incoming thought rushes by unrebuked, it will consider it an invitation to barge in. In order to get rid of that thought, it must be repented of. The longer a destructive or sinful thought is allowed to stay, the less effect your rebuke will have. Rebuking thoughts works at the front gate, not in the basement! Start checking your thought life, and you will find yourself rebuking the enemy daily and repenting of things you had forgotten about that are living in your spirit. Set up a checkpoint where all thoughts must stop before gaining access into your mind.

*O Jerusalem, wash thine heart from wickedness, that thou mayest be saved. How long shall thy vain thoughts lodge within thee?* (Jer. 4:14)

## DON'T FORGET TO FORGIVE

Once a destructive thought is removed, it must be replaced with its equal: anger must be replaced with gentleness; panic must be replaced by trust; the distraction must be replaced by the word.

Repentance can resolve every issue, and it begins in the thought life. Above all, remember to forgive, because forgiveness is a significant part of repentance. Sometimes the greatest repenting we can do is actually forgiving someone.

I'm learning that the longer the wound has festered, the greater the act of forgiveness must be. For example, some people might just need an "I'm sorry for what I said," while others might need a blessing to go along with the apology (e.g., financial or some other kindness). (See Romans 12:17–21 on overcoming evil with good.) Giving is part of forgiving, and sometimes we need to go beyond apology and bless the person we are forgiving. It is very difficult to hold a grudge against someone that you bless, especially if they receive the blessing with thankfulness. The point is that forgiveness must replace hatred in our thoughts if it is ever going to change anything or anyone that we are dealing with in our world.

Forgiveness not only can heal sickness of the mind and emotions, it also can help heal sicknesses in the body. Oftentimes people suffer great inward pain, especially in the stomach region of the body, when there is an unresolved issue with another person in their life. The contrast is striking: there is life and healing in forgiveness, but there is death and infirmity in unforgiveness.

## FASTING FORCES FORGIVENESS

One reason why fasting is powerful is that it forces forgiveness; that is, it will force forgiveness if the motive of the fast is launched in true humility. If there is an unresolved issue with a brother, we are instructed to lay down the sacrifice we were bringing to God and go make things right with our brother. Fasting will bring heart issues to the surface so the balm of a humble action can begin the healing process. Fasting demands grudges to be replaced with grace, hatred to be replaced by humility, and bitterness to be replaced by blessing.

Replacing negative thoughts with positive ones is easier said than done, but it is possible if you will train your mind to become a conduit of praise instead a conduit of pain. Learn the art of teaching your mind to praise the Lord even before your mouth does. A person who is constantly praising God in their mind is very difficult for the enemy to defeat. People who praise God in their mind think themselves happy, as Paul did in Acts 26. If you are having trouble training your mind to be positive and happy, perhaps the following instruction by Paul will help you develop a strategy that works.

> *Finally, brethren, whatsoever things are true, whatsoever things are honest, whatsoever things are just, whatsoever things are pure, whatsoever things are lovely, whatsoever things are of good report; if there be any virtue, and if there be any praise, think on these things.* (Phil. 4:8)

## THE RESULT OF A GOD THOUGHT

Ultimately, you need to desire to dwell in the dimension of living out God's thoughts for your future. Believe it or not, God thinks about you all day, every day. Yes, you are that special to him and he has huge plans for your life, plans you might not know about yet. If you can rebuke the thoughts of hell that are trying to invade your present and repent of the thoughts that have dwelt in the basement of your past, you can replace them with thoughts of your future. Those thoughts can come only from your creator.

*For I know the thoughts that I think toward you, saith the Lord, thoughts of peace, and not of evil, to give you an expected end.* (Jer. 29:11)

The last phrase of this verse astounds me. God's thoughts toward us are sent to give us an expected end. In the original Hebrew, the word "expected" is tiqvah, meaning cord, hope, things hoped for, and outcome. If one of those definitions sounds familiar, perhaps Hebrews 11:1 comes to mind: "Faith is the substance of things hoped for, the evidence of things not seen." Apparently, faith is hoping for something and expecting it to happen. Even more astounding, if this verse is combined with Jeremiah 29:11, we realize that if we have faith for something that is the will of God for our lives, what we are calling "faith" is actually a thought from God regarding our future!

Need more clarity? God thinks a thought about you and your future. He drops that thought toward you and suddenly you start having faith that this God thought will happen. In other words, your faith is a product of the thoughts of God. The result is whatever you are believing God for. Fasting with faith is simply saying, "God, I want your thoughts for my life so desperately that I will put anything and everything aside to get them!" Nothing else matters more than having his thoughts become your reality. Fasting makes that happen.

Everything you desire to be for the Lord and everything you desire to see him do in your life is available through the avenue of fasting. Fasting tells your thoughts that you are inadequate, but someone much more than adequate can make your dreams come true for his kingdom. Fasting is a castle-crushing machine, and hell fears it immensely. Fasting shifts your thought patterns from dwelling on your past to envisioning your future!

You will find it is difficult for your mind to stay focused on how bad the past has been when you make your body fast for something in store in your future. Fasting truly transforms the mind. It releases endorphins (positive hormones) and not cortisol (negative hormones). You'll be excited instead of depressed because the undercurrent of discouragement has been ripped out and your thoughts are launching you up to the clouds of destiny.

Fasting will permeate your speech and ultimately your thought life. Fasting causes impulsive reactions to be calmed by the Spirit of the Lord. Fasting long enough will take you out of carnal thinking and carnal speaking and connect you to thoughts from the mind of God and words of life. Fasting reveals what is lying dormant in the basement of your soul and demands that you take action.

Fasting removes the clutter of carnal thinking and reveals the treasure of a triumphant thought life. There is no greater victory to be won than that in the thought life. Fasting will force the issue and make you change the way you think and therefore speak. There isn't a place in your life that is deep enough to hide from a fast. Fasting will literally search the crevices of your life and reveal every thought that has become a brick in the stronghold within.

The fortress that has been built in your mind can be destroyed only by a focused invasion. Fasting is the battering ram that knocks the gate down and charges the enemy. It is good to fast until every thought is forced to submit to the will of God for your life. Your stomach will tell your mind early on in the fast that there's no point to this and you should just give up and eat. Your mind will contemplate it, but the power of fasting will take those thoughts into captivity because something greater is at stake—your destiny!

Fasting will disconnect you from what you were and connect you to what you were meant to be. Just ask the apostle Paul.

He did not simply leave the world of violence and step into a ministry of victory. In between leaving who he was and becoming what he was meant to be there was a three-day fast without food or water. His future, his vision, and his destiny depended on the three-day window in which he would deny his flesh of the very source it depended on for survival. Sometimes it takes a conversion and a fast to really step into your future.

Fasting causes the stagnant waters of the present to be cleansed by the current of the future. When believers enter a fast, hope begins to breathe into their heart. What they're going through somehow will be altered by what they're connecting to on this fast.

There is a resiliency for your future that can be restored only through extended fasting. If you are feeling that you have reached the pinnacle of God's plan for your life and are now in the mental position of descent, it is time to go on a fast.

Fasting is leaving the earth in your spirit to approach the throne room of the King of kings to release your petition. Your body remains on the earth and feels the effect of the lack of earthly comfort, but your spirit is soaring into the heavens expecting a divine breakthrough. Fasting is indeed approaching the king with an unstoppable desperation that demands response. Fasting declares, "I might die, but I will get an audience with the ruler before I do." Ask Esther, who said, "Somehow I'm going to get in that throne room to state my request, and if I perish, I perish!"

Hell hates and fears the power of petitioning. The strongest complaint Daniel's adversaries had against him was that he offered petitions to God three times a day. They weren't upset just because he prayed, but rather they were upset about when he prayed—which was multiple times a day. In the throne room, fasting is petitioning for a need over and over. It drives the enemy crazy. Want an answer? Go on a fasting petition quest!

# CHAPTER 12

# A Mission Worth Fasting For

Hell's greatest nightmare is a child of God on a mission. A person with a made-up mind to stand in the gap and make a difference in the kingdom of God is considered a threat among demons. Conversely, people who sit idly by, thinking to coast into heaven on the coattails of the consecration of others don't trouble the enemy at all. No mission, no threat.

One of the greatest missions ever recorded in scripture is found in the book of Nehemiah. Despite living a comfortable life as a cupbearer to King Artaxerxes in the Persian palace at Shushan, something was amiss for Nehemiah. Years prior, his hometown of Jerusalem had suffered a great misfortune; the walls had been reduced to rubble and the gates had been burned to the ground, leaving the inhabitants defenseless. The majority of the population living there when it was taken had either been captured or killed by Nebuchadnezzar, king of Babylon. Now their children and grandchildren were living there under heavy reproach and affliction.

The day Nehemiah realized his people were suffering, his world darkened. He was no longer content with his cushy position in the palace. He was no longer satisfied to just "serve the world" when there was a world he could save.

Quick question to the reader: Does your mission involve serving the world, or saving the world? I don't mean if you're not preaching that you're not reaching; I mean are you reaching anyone, anywhere? Are you burdened for a coworker or are you just there to do your job and get a paycheck? A mission from God keeps you praying, crying, and hoping for a miracle breakthrough. A mission from God will motivate you to consecrate. A divine mission comes with a heavy burden and a dependency on God to stand in the gap that your intelligence, wisdom, personality, finances, looks, and charisma cannot fill. If God doesn't help, the mission will fail. That's why I call it a divine mission. It requires God's guidance and constant involvement if the mission is to succeed.

Nehemiah knew his position in the palace didn't give him enough leverage to help rebuild Jerusalem's walls. Even with a stamp of approval from his sovereign, he knew a mission of that magnitude would require divine favor. If it was going to succeed, he needed heavenly authorization. Nehemiah knew how to get God's attention: he immediately went on a fast.

I hope you caught that last sentence because nothing has changed. If you believe God is sending you on a mission, go on a fast to confirm the authorization. If you feel God calling you to a mission, fasting will be the signature on the orders you're receiving. It either confirms your mission is in the will of God and gives you the green light, or it gives you the red light, and you need to stop and wait. You may have heard the call to mission, but it might be the wrong timing for your expedition.

Nehemiah fasted because of the pain he felt for the suffering people in his beloved Jerusalem. His answer would be if the king signed off on Nehemiah's desire to go rebuild the walls. Fasting out of pain often leads to fasting for a purpose. You're not just hoping God will move; you're hoping he will connect you to the miracle and let you be a part of the restoration.

After Nehemiah secured his heavenly king's authorization to go on the mission, it didn't take long for the Persian king to follow suit. Proverbs 21:1 tells us that the heart of the king is in the hand of the Lord. If God authorizes your mission, no earthly power will be able to stand against his decision. His word will not return unto him void. It will accomplish the mission on which it is sent.

Whether or not Nehemiah expected immediate results at this point, he realized that fasting can make missions happen immediately. He was seeing firsthand that when a person fasts, he gets the confidence that the will of man will surrender to the will of God, and God's will surely will be accomplished. Artaxerxes commissioned Nehemiah to go check out the broken-down walls of Jerusalem and authorized him to rebuild them. To bring the illustration close to home, fasting will get you more results than you dreamed!

Although Nehemiah's mission wouldn't be easy, it had been preapproved by the king. Fasting will get things preapproved for your destiny despite the enormity of the opposition. The enemy was set on aborting Nehemiah's mission, but the mission had already been authorized by a higher power. The next time hell tries to abort what you feel to do for God, remind the enemy that you are on a divine mission that has been preapproved by the king eternal. The mission God has planned for your life is going to manifest only after you fast your way into faith that you are truly chosen to accomplish it.

## QUESTIONS FROM HELL

When hell learned about Nehemiah's mission, it summoned two powerful opponents in an effort to stop all progress on the part of the Jews. These opponents were Sanballat and Tobiah. According to the Elephantine Papyri (a collection of ancient documents from the fifth century BC), Sanballat was governor of Samaria. His daughter was married to the grandson of Jerusalem's high priest (Neh. 13:28), indicating powerful connections in Judah. Sanballat was a Moabite and apparently had inherited the hatred Moab had for the Jews. Sanballat controlled two key cities on the trade route and therefore had the power to do the Jews great harm economically.

Tobiah, an Ammonite, also harbored hatred for Nehemiah and his mission. Tobiah had the authority of Persia behind him, as it is thought that Medo-Persian authorities had appointed him governor of Ammon. He was married to a Jewish woman and was in high favor with Eliashib, the high priest at Jerusalem. In addition, many in Judah were "sworn to him" (Neh. 6:17–18) because his son, Johanan, was married to the daughter of Meshullam, a man who assisted Nehemiah in repairing the wall (Neh. 3:4). Unfortunately, these familial connections did nothing to temper his hatred of Nehemiah and what he was attempting to accomplish for the Lord.

Sanballat and Tobiah were "very displeased that someone had come to help the people of Israel" (Neh. 2:10, NLT). They despised Nehemiah and laughed him and those "feeble Jews" to scorn. When you arrive on the scene of your potential destiny, hell will immediately begin mocking you. If hell senses you are isolated upon arrival, it will intimidate you, hoping you'll give up before you even begin. Therefore, I contend you need to know not only what God is asking of you, but also what the enemy is asking about you.

Common questions you will hear from the Lord at the time of your mission launch might sound like these: Will you go? Will you fast? Will you stay the course and not look back? Will you trust me? Will you submit to my will? It is vital to the success of your mission that you answer these questions before you begin.

Next, we will delve into five big questions the enemy posed at the onset of Nehemiah's mission. These, of course, were part of Sanballat's taunting and were meant to dissuade Nehemiah from his mission.

## WHAT DO THESE FEEBLE JEWS?

The five questions from Sanballat's speech to the Samaritan chiefs and military leaders are found in Nehemiah 4:2. The first question was not "What do you think you're doing, Nehemiah?" or "What do you think these Samaritan soldiers will do to you?" The question was, "What are these feeble Jews doing?" In other words, hell wants to know if your mission involves the weak people near you, which would give the enemy an easy win. We know you're on a mission, but is your mission for you alone or are others going to be involved? Not just any old others—others who are neither skilled nor strong. We know you have a plan for the brilliant, but do you have a plan for the broken? It seems the enemy's immediate concern about any God-ordained mission is whether the leader will involve the ones no one believes in. Anyone can invest in potential greatness, but can you see greatness in those who are neither skilled nor strong? It is easy to motivate the dreamer, but can you motivate the damaged?

These "feeble Jews" were the remnant—people King Nebu-chadnezzar had thought too worthless to be taken captive during the Babylonian invasion of Judah. Nebuchadnezzar didn't antici-pate any uprising from this remnant because they lacked the po-tential to rebuild Jerusalem physically, financially, and agricultur-ally; Babylon had simply left them there to die. These feeble Jews had somehow survived and raised children and grandchildren, who now inhabited a city with no walls, no protection, no great success or importance, and seemingly no means of getting any of those things. In hell's eyes, the feeble are merely weak survivors.

What hell doesn't realize is that survivors can become their worst nightmare. There is nothing more dangerous in a city than a God-called, ordained leader fasting for revival and survivors, feeble though they may be, attaching themselves to the leader's endeavor. When you've already been through the worst of the worst, yet you're standing and believing God still has plans for your life, your very existence displeases hell.

Survivors have tenacity; they hold on and don't quit. They don't give in when times get tough. Simply put, if Satan's forces know you're a survivor, they worry because it will take a lot to take you out. If the survivors get involved in Nehemiah's mission, it will get accomplished—and heaven and hell both know it!

## WILL THEY FORTIFY THEMSELVES?

Sanballat's second question was not "How could these fee-ble Jews possibly think they have the strength—much less the means—to restore the wall by themselves?" but "Will they get to the place where they learn to strengthen themselves?" The enemy knew that if these Jews summoned the courage and strength to withstand the ridicule and other evil tactics, it would make a drastic difference in the outcome of the mission. When people learn to encourage themselves, they suddenly become weapons, even when they're standing alone.

Hell knows that when you hear your pastor preach or you're around the body of Christ, you will receive encouragement and strength. But people who encourage themselves walk in a different strength. For example, David knew how to encourage himself. Even when he had lost his family and his own men wanted to kill him, he tapped into a place in God where he could increase his strength without any help. The Bible says David encouraged himself in the Lord. This is something hell fears! My friend, stir up the gift that is within you. Don't wait for others to strengthen you; strengthen yourself in the Lord.

Self-encouragement kills self-entitlement. When David encouraged himself in the Lord, he placed himself in a position to request something from God. He asked if he should pursue the enemy, and if he pursued, would he overtake them? What he did not ask was, "Shall I recover all?" But when God answered, he informed David that he indeed should pursue, that he would overtake the enemy and recover all. The Lord granted him an even greater level of favor simply because he didn't ask for it. If he would have asked to recover all of their belongings, he still would have been operating in entitlement. His humility in not asking for anything other than victory in the battle released God to give David more than mere victory; he gave him the spoils of war.

As Paul stood bound in chains, beaten, and bloodied before a king who had a legacy of murder, things were looking rather dim. What was the king's legacy of murder? Agrippa's great-grandfather was Herod the Great, the king who had ordered the slaughter of all of Bethlehem's babies around the time Jesus was born (Matt. 2:16). His grandfather was Herod Antipas, who had ordered the beheading of John the Baptist (Matt. 14:1–12). His father, Agrippa I, was responsible for James's death (Acts 12). Paul now stood before Herod Agrippa II as a prisoner who could face the same fate as the previous heroes, yet he boldly declared, "I think myself happy." He was, in effect, saying, "No matter what you do to me on the outside, in my mind I have you pinned on the mat because I've learned to encourage myself." What a revelation! Learning how to strengthen yourself will strike fear into the heart of the adversary every time.

## WILL THEY SACRIFICE?

Sanballat's third question astounds me, because it's a question I wouldn't expect the enemy to ask. It seems to me the question "Will they sacrifice?" normally would come from God or a spiritual leader. But here we have the adversary asking about sacrifice. The question was not "Will Nehemiah sacrifice?" but "Will they sacrifice?" The enemy knew Nehemiah was committed to sacrifice because of the single-mindedness he displayed in executing the mission. The enemy wanted to know if the others were just as serious as Nehemiah.

I believe that if any church is going to experience the revival they desire, they have to believe in corporate sacrifice, not just leadership sacrifice. The difference between a church where only the leaders sacrifice and a church where everyone fasts, everyone gives to missions, everyone prays, and everyone goes on outreach is astronomical.

The impact on a city or community is limited when only the pastor fasts, prays, and gives his all. I believe you can have a greater revival if your entire church fasts for three days than you will have if one person fasts for thirty days. Here's why: the one who fasts thirty days is destined to reap most of the rewards because they themselves are doing the sacrificing. However, when a group of people is inspired to fast for an answer, the results multiply and are manifested throughout the church, the city, and the community.

Is this church waiting for God to send them answers, or are they willing to kill some things in order to receive the answers? Are they ready to die so that they might live? Will they sacrifice? Hell is not intimidated at all by a church that is stuck in the waiting game with God. Churches that seem to never have revival are the ones that always appear to be waiting for it to show up. However, revival seems to be continually manifesting in churches that will sacrifice for it. Simply put, if everyone sacrifices, hell will instantly be worried about what heaven will send to that church in response to the sacrifice! Heaven will invade atmospheres where there are sacrifices on the altar. Favor will find the fast-ers. Blessings seem to always trickle down to those who sacrificially bless others.

The opposite also is true: where there is no sacrifice, there will rarely be heavenly favor. Just ask Cain. Cain thought sacrifice to the Lord was no big deal. He soon found out otherwise, but rather than humble himself and submit to God's advice, he chose to murder the one sacrificing—his brother, Abel. Often those who refuse to sacrifice will feel conviction and take up issues with those who do. When conviction hits them, though, there is a decision that must be made: either humble yourself or cause a scene. Cain chose the latter. He found out it didn't pay off in the end.

## WILL THEY MAKE AN END IN A DAY?

This question, "Will they make an end in a day?" appears to have a dual motive behind it. Sanballat and his cronies not only were wondering if it was possible for the people to get this wall rebuilt quickly, but also if they would quit if their mission wasn't accomplished quickly. Hell wanted to know if it was possible that the feeble Jews could quickly restore something so shattered and broken. Further, the enemy was wondering if the people of God would stay on track if the mission took longer than they expected. Sanballat and his crew were itching to implement their plans to hinder and delay the project.

Perhaps my question to you is, are you going to last if the outcome doesn't happen when you think it should or the way it should? Will you stay focused on your destiny when it appears to be farther away than you originally estimated? The Christian Standard Bible asks the question this way: "Will they ever finish it?" Hell wants you to believe that what the Lord started in you will never reach completion because of all the delays you are experiencing!

In the spirit world the signal that you are headed in the right direction toward your destiny is not favor, but rather, resistance. For instance, we tend to think Joseph was on his way to his destiny when God reversed the course of his life and he stepped out of the prison gate and into the palace. On the contrary, Joseph was officially on the way to his destiny when his coat of many colors was stripped off and he was thrown into a pit. Arriving at his destiny took much longer than he probably expected, but by living daily in the dimension of servanthood he was silencing the voices of the enemy that were sneering, "Will he ever finish? Will he ever come out of this?" The answer was a resounding "Yes!" and so is your answer. You will make an end in a day!

## WILL THEY REVIVE THE STONES OUT OF THE HEAPS OF BURNED RUBBISH?

Embedded in this question is a gold mine full of nuggets of revelation for your soul. Let's mine a few of these treasures. First, the question begins, "Will they revive the stones?" These stones were what was left of the burned-down wall that been demolished under the siege of Babylon seventy years prior. The question was not if they would bring in new stones, but rather, "Do they plan on using the stones that used to be in this wall?" There wouldn't be an incoming inventory of freshly hewn rocks to rebuild Jerusalem's wall; they planned to use the broken and burned stones that had been in the original wall. I believe there is a major harvest of backsliders and lost loved ones coming back to the wall, and hell is nervous about it.

Where were these stones? They were everywhere—lying in heaps of unsightly trash and rubble. Where was all this trash? Still in the city! The broken are still hovering near the wall. There are people who used to come to church but now their lives are broken and burned—but they are still living in town. Hell wants to know if you plan on contacting them. Do you plan on lifting them up, dusting them off, and finding a place for them in the wall? Is there a spot in your church, in your youth group, in your hyphen crew for a broken and burned rock that's been languishing for years in the trash? Are you fasting for your own destiny, or are you looking to restore those who are languishing in the dump, but their hearts are crying from the fire of life's pain, "Please send me a Nehemiah!

Send me someone who fasts long enough to get a burden for all of my family, not just me."

Your influence multiplies when your consecration and motives are selfless. Hell is worried you will discover the answer you really need is closer than you think. It is just camouflaged in ashes and chaos. The blemished stones will acquire value only if a consecrated someone is willing to pick them up, dust them off, and find a place for them in the wall!

Nehemiah 4:7 records that the breaches in the wall were beginning to be stopped, or as the New International Version states, "the gaps were being closed." What were they using to fill in the gaps? The broken, blemished, busted-up stones. People with nothing to lose can fill in the gaps like no one else. People who never should have come through what they endured can be breach blockers. Nehemiah fasted for others, then restored their broken pieces and repaired their wall. No enemy—no Sanballat or Tobiah or any of their henchmen—could stop that mission because it was ordained by the King of kings, and it was launched by fasting.

The enemy fears when your fast becomes contagious. When your motive for fasting is the revival of others, you are officially fasting forward. So go ahead, launch your fast. Don't worry about obstacles, hindrances, and enemies. The Lord said at the Red Sea, "Tell the people to go forward." He is now saying it again! It is time to fast. It is time to Fast Forward. Make this your life's motto: If you pray hard, dream big, and fast long, you will be given a divine mission from the Lord. So keep on reading, keep on praying, and launch your fast.

Made in the USA
Monee, IL
25 January 2022

89834100R00095